JEREMIAH: A PARABLE OF JESUS

OTHER BOOKS BY DOUG WEBSTER

The Easy Yoke NavPress 1995

The Discipline of Surrender: Biblical Images of Discipleship IVP 20001

The Living Word: Ten Life-Changing Ways to Experience the Bible Moody 2003

Under the Radar: A Conversation on Spiritual Leadership Regent College 2007

Selling Jesus: What's Wrong with Marketing the Church Wipf & Stock 2009

JEREMIAH:
A PARABLE OF JESUS

DOUGLAS D. WEBSTER

SOLID GROUND CHRISTIAN BOOKS
BIRMINGHAM, ALABAMA USA

Solid Ground Christian Books
PO Box 660132
Vestavia Hills AL 35266
205-443-0311
sgcb@charter.net
solid-ground-books.com

JEREMIAH: A Parable of Jesus
by Douglas D. Webster

First Solid Ground Edition August 2009

SPECIAL THANKS – from the author and publisher
To Susan Montoya for her creative work on the cover
To Jim Meals for editorial assistance

Cover design by Susan Montoya, Chula Vista, CA

ISBN: 978-159925-218-6

To our son Jeremiah
who stands in the tradition of the prophet

TABLE OF CONTENTS

Foreword

Six hundred years before Jesus, God called Jeremiah to be a prophet. When we place the life of Jeremiah alongside Jesus, in much the same way that a parable is told alongside truth, our understanding of what it means to follow Jesus deepens. Ever since I was sixteen Jeremiah's life has had an impact on me. I identified with Jeremiah because he was called to be a prophet when he was only a teenager and then for the next forty years he challenged the religious and political systems with such courage and sacrifice. I can picture Jeremiah in my mind's eye delivering his Temple Sermon with holy abandon. There is a remarkable immediacy about his life and message that I find convicting—compelling. His actions are bold; his feelings raw, and he keeps on doing what the Lord wants him to do regardless of the consequences. For any follower of Jesus, young or old, that is impressive.

Larger-than-life personalities can take on iconic status, becoming symbols that mirror back to people their hopes and dreams. Like the flag or the Queen or a celebrity they represent what we want them to represent. But not the prophet Jeremiah. Instead of standing like a mannequin dressed in conventional religious thought,

Jeremiah lived as a parable of Jesus causing us to think long and hard of what it means to take God's Word seriously. Parables come at the truth indirectly, provocatively, even subversively. Symbols reinforce our thinking about religion, but parables are designed to make us think about what it means to follow Jesus.

The Book of Jeremiah challenges the status quo, pulls the rug out from our preconceived religious notions and demands authentic obedience—no matter what the cost. If you want to keep your life intact, Jeremiah is not a safe person to study. Jeremiah makes enemies of those who resist the will of God, but he is a soul-mate to all who seek a passion for Christ. His Gethsemane life guides today's disciples in living for Christ and His Kingdom. The best way to read this book is with the Bible open before you. The aim is simple, to prompt a closer reading of the prophet Jeremiah and a deeper commitment to the Lord Jesus.

1. The Call

"See, today I appoint you over nations and kingdoms to uproot and tear down, to destroy and overthrow, to build and to plant." Jeremiah 1:10

If we are tired of the mundane, ho-hum religious life, we could pick no better guide to lead us out of the doldrums than Jeremiah. As he grew older, his life did not shrink, it expanded. Instead of becoming feeble and frail, self-absorbed and petty, he continued to be as God promised, like a fortified city, an iron pillar and a bronze wall (1:18). Jerusalem's kings capitulated, her people gave in to every form of evil, and her prophets deceived, but Jeremiah persisted in living and proclaiming the Word of the Lord. Jeremiah did not live an easy life, but he lived an intensely meaningful life.

Of all the prophets, Jeremiah's life illustrated the message he communicated. He incarnated the truth he was called of God to deliver. He lived better than he knew. Long before the Word was made flesh and dwelt among us, Jeremiah embodied the Gethsemane mind-set, took up his cross and lived in the hope of the resurrection. Isaiah prophesied that the suffering Servant would be led "like a lamb to the slaughter" (Isa.53:7) and John the Baptist proclaimed boldly, "Behold the Lamb of God who takes away the sin of the world," but it was Jeremiah who felt like a gentle lamb led to the slaughter (11:19). The complexities and tensions that the prophet Jeremiah experienced are not unlike the pressures and trials facing today's followers of Christ. If you are fed up with Christianity without Christ, tired of ego-centric pastors, overwhelmed with the challenges of living for Christ in a secular society and confused by the array of popular spiritualities, let Jeremiah be your Spirit-inspired guide.

Everyone seems to find the Book of Jeremiah confusing, but a few pointers may make it easier. The fact that the book is not laid out like the alphabet drives linear thinkers to distraction. We like things neatly arranged in sequential order, but this biblical book does not go from A-Z. These fifty-two chapters are a collection of high impact images designed to impress the reader with the Word of the Lord from every angle. Detailing *when* Jeremiah said what he did is not nearly as important as what he said and where he said it. In one sense the political chronology is incidental to Jeremiah, but the substance of what Jeremiah communicated is absolutely vital. The book of Jeremiah may be an historian's nightmare, but it is a communicator's master-piece. The message rules. Biting critiques that spiral into tornadoes of truth, judgment pronouncements that fall like hammer blows, soul-searching confessions and tear-driven lamentations, all add up to a powerful message.

We never really finish reading the Book of Jeremiah, nor were we meant to. The message doesn't end when Judah is forced into exile or when King Zedekiah dies, because the force of the prophecy was meant to be enduring until Christ comes again—for the second time. The history that mattered to Jeremiah was Salvation History. He was fully aware that kings come and go and empires rise and fall, but it was the Word of the Lord that endured forever. That was what impressed him and should impress us. Born about 645 BC he preached 600 years before Jesus, but his Christ-centered preaching is still vital today. His God-inspired Word teaches us how to follow Jesus today.

The Revealing Prophet

More than any other prophet, Jeremiah revealed his heart and soul. The human side of working out the divine calling is on every page. It is evident in the on-going dialogue between the Lord and Jeremiah. Jeremiah was not afraid to express his feelings and confront his fears. He lashed out in hot anger against his enemies and complained bitterly to the Lord. He disclosed the plots and betrayals, slander and ridicule that were directed against him, because he delivered an unpopular message. From his calling in 627 BC, during the reign of Josiah, to the fall of Jerusalem in 587 BC, Jeremiah never stopped proclaiming the Word of the Lord, even though it was met with constant opposition. Like Job, Jeremiah cursed the day of his birth, but in the same breath claimed that the Lord was with him like a mighty warrior and that all his persecutors were destined for disgrace (20:11-18). In the eyes of the world, Jeremiah was a failure, but in the eyes of God, he was the prophet who personally came closest to revealing his one and only son's path to the Cross.

Jeremiah was the son of a priest named Hilkiah from Anathoth, a small town three miles east of Jerusalem. The name "Hilkiah," like the name "Jeremiah," was a common name in those days, which explains why most scholars conclude that Jeremiah's father was not Hilkiah the high priest in Jerusalem who discovered the Book of the Law (2 Kings 22:8). Names meant something back then, but not everyone lived up to their name. Josiah (639-609 BC) meant "God heals." Jehoiakim (609-597 BC) meant "the Lord raises up" and Zedekiah (597-587 BC) meant "the Lord is righteous." There was a double meaning associated with Jeremiah's name. It could mean "the Lord exalts" or it could mean "the Lord hurls." Forty years of prophetic ministry proved that no one was better suited for his name than Jeremiah.

We are all shaped to some degree by our time and place, but these factors may not be the most important influences upon us. Hopefully they are not. Our lives were meant to be shaped by God. For Jeremiah, life was defined, not by culture and circumstances, but by the Word of the Lord. This is the singular truth that constantly impresses us about Jeremiah. "The Word of the Lord came to him in the thirteenth year of the reign of Josiah..." and it never stopped coming to him (1:2). "The Word of the Lord came to me," was the self-perceived truth that defined him personally, set his agenda publicly, and determined the entire course of his life. Jeremiah shows us what it means to be shaped, guided, nurtured, transformed, and empowered by the Word of God. His personal story was part of God's great Salvation History story. The life issues addressed in the first chapter are the issues that we all struggle with: self-understanding, personal significance, feelings of inadequacy, meaning and purpose, disruptive times, life-threatening circumstances and the courage to persevere. For Jeremiah, it was the Word of the Lord, that helped him deal with each one of these issues, not just for the moment but for his entire life.

When the Word of the Lord defines who we are and what we do, we can't help but take notice of what the Lord is doing to us, for us, in us and around us. In his dialogue with the Lord, Jeremiah repeatedly heard the promise and the call: "I formed you...I knew you...I set you apart...I appointed you ...You must go to everyone I send you and say whatever I command you...I am with you and will rescue you...I have put my words in your mouth....I appoint you over nations and kingdoms ...I have made you a fortified city, an iron pillar and a bronze wall...I am with you and will rescue you," declares the Lord.

The Personhood of All Believers

One thing is certain, Jeremiah was not a self-made person. His identify, purpose, significance and calling came from the Lord. All too often, we think of God as the object and ourselves as the subject. We suppose God is the passive object of our inquiry and debate, and the quiet recipient of our apathy or adoration or anger. But as Jeremiah knew so well, it is really the other way around. God's first-person action defined him. "Before Jeremiah knew God, God knew Jeremiah: 'Before I formed you in the womb I knew you.' This turns everything we ever thought about God around."[i] The ego-centric approach is really laughable when you think about it. Who are we to sit in judgment on God and debate whether God is an illusion or a myth or a figment of our imagination? It is the myth of human self-sufficiency that ought to be exposed. Our significance lies in God's action, not in our achievement, and only when this is grasped in the depth of our souls does our action become meaningful.

The Word of the Lord came to me, saying,
"Before **I formed you** in the womb
I knew you,
before you were born **I set you** apart;
I appointed you as a prophet to the nations."

Jeremiah's life did not begin with Jeremiah. It began with God, the God who created him, commended him, consecrated and commissioned him. And all of this happened long before he was aware of himself, realized his need, or longed for significance. Without diminishing the uniqueness of this truth for Jeremiah, what was said of Jeremiah is true for all of us. "In the beginning God...." works not only for the universe, but for each one of us personally (Gen.1:1). We were all meant to hear the Word of the Lord saying to us, "I created you, I understand you, and I alone can save you and give you significance." This is what makes Jeremiah especially important for those who follow the Lord Jesus. "God's call to Jeremiah to be a prophet parallels his call to us to be a person."[ii]

King David's prayer is true for all people, because all people are created in God's image:

"For you created my inmost being; you knit me together in my mother's womb. I praise you because I am fearfully and wonderfully made...Your eyes saw my unformed body. All the days ordained for me were written in your book before one of them came to be. How precious to me are your thoughts, O God! How vast is the sum of them!" (Ps.139:13-14, 16).

The value of human life is not found in the will of parents or in self-achievement, but in the will of God. Human worth is not a matter of human potential but of divine principle. If the value of life is determined by what we make of it then existence precedes essence, but if the value of human life is determined by the will and Word of God then essence precedes existence. Life is not a matter of what we achieve but of what we receive from God. This is why abortion is wrong and the plight of starving children everywhere is tragic. This is why the human embryo cannot be treated as experimental tissue and this is why human life is guarded with capital punishment. The Word of the Lord that came to Jeremiah comes to us and reminds us that we are created in God's image; God is not created in our image.

We can identify with Jeremiah because he shows us what it is to be a person created, known, set apart and called by the Sovereign Lord. We can learn from his example because he shows us how to live through difficult times. "In looking for a companion who has lived through catastrophic disruption and survived with grace, biblical people more often than not come upon Jeremiah and receive him as a true, honest, and God-revealing companion for the worst of times."[iii]

Many believers identify with Jeremiah in terms of being "formed", "known" and "set apart" but they consider the fourth divine action ("I appointed you as a prophet to the nations") as strictly applied to Jeremiah, with the possible exception of ordained ministers who proclaim the Word or cross-cultural missionaries who deliver the gospel to the nations. But this fourth description of the call is as relevant as the first three provisions. Like Jeremiah, all those who follow the Lord Jesus Christ are called to the nations. The Bible's teaching on the priesthood of all believers opens up the powerful example of Jeremiah's life to the follower of Jesus. If we consider our lives in the stream of salvation history, Jeremiah is not only an ancient prophet but a prototype disciple.

The day that Moses longed for and the prophet Joel anticipated has arrived in Christ. There was an incident in the wilderness that provoked a particularly revealing comment from Moses. When the Spirit of God came upon the seventy elders who had been appointed to help Moses lead, they prophesied. But two elders, Eldad and Medad, who stayed back in the camp also prophesied. This disturbed Joshua who saw the incident as a threat to the chain of command. He excitedly appealed to his superior saying, "Moses, my lord, stop them!" But Moses replied, "Are you jealous for my sake? I wish that all the Lord's people were prophets and the Lord would put his Spirit on them!" (Num.11:28-29).

Centuries later, Joel prophesied what would happen on the Day of the Lord. Thus says the Lord, "I will pour out my Spirit on all people. Your sons and daughters will prophesy, your old men will dream dreams, your young men will see visions....And everyone who calls on the name of the Lord will be saved..." (Joel 2:28,32). This is the prophecy that the apostle Peter declared to be fulfilled on the day of Pentecost when the Holy Spirit came upon the disciples and they began to speak in other tongues (Acts 2). And this is the truth that lies behind the great commission that Jesus gave after his resurrection and before his ascension to all believers: "Therefore go and make disciples of all nations, baptizing them in the name of the Father and of the Son and of the Holy Spirit, and teaching them to obey everything I have commanded you. And surely I will be with you always, to the very end of the age" (Matt.28:19-20).

The priesthood of all believers and the shared mandate of the Great Commission open up the fullness of Jeremiah's example to us. He is our companion, guide and mentor in being the person that God calls us to be and in proclaiming the Word of the Lord entrusted to us. Furthermore, Jeremiah shows us that being a person and being a prophet are really one in the same, because we are not called to merely say something, we are called to live out the message in the fullness of life. Thus, the *personhood of all believers* turns Jeremiah's life into a vital example for us.

What then is the first lesson that Jeremiah teaches us? What was his first reaction to the call of God? What would you have said if you were Jeremiah? How would you have responded to being God-created, God-known, God-consecrated and God-commissioned? *You* were meant to be more like Jeremiah than you ever imagined.

Jeremiah opened his mouth and said, "Ah, Sovereign Lord, I do not know how to speak; I am only a child."

The first thing out of his mouth was an excuse, not a rebellious, obstinate excuse, but a "sorry-I'm-inadequate" excuse. It was "the cry of weakness, not of unwillingness."[iv] "I am only a boy," was his excuse. He used his age, probably around eighteen years old, and his inexperience and his feelings of inadequacy as an excuse. What's yours? "I am only a housewife." "I am only a high school student." "I am only a business person." I wonder if the prophet Jeremiah came to mind when the apostle Paul challenged Timothy, saying, "Don't let anyone look down on you because you are young, but set an example for the believers in speech, in life, in love, in faith and in purity" (1 Tim.4:12). Like Jeremiah, we are tempted to allow our self-definition to shape and control our lives. We have to be coached and challenged out of our depreciating self-talk by the Word of the Lord. We have to stop saying, "I am only..." and start realizing what God has done, is doing and will do in us and for us.

The Lord's response to Jeremiah's fear of inadequacy goes beyond instructing him and redirects us as well. What follows is a case study in spiritual direction, a solid example of divine therapy designed to remove the emotional and spiritual obstacles that get in the way of obeying God's call. It is essential counsel that is worth remembering and applying often, because we have a natural bent to hide behind excuses.

The Lord's counsel starts out simple and direct: "But the Lord said to me, 'Do not say, 'I am only a child.' There is no mystery in being told to stop. It is as clear as a bright red, hexagonal traffic sign. Out of necessity the negative inner monologue must cease and be replaced by the Word of the Lord. God's *no*, "Do not say..." was followed immediately by God's *yes*. Jeremiah was faced with God's absolute imperative, "You must go to everyone I send you to and say whatever I command you" (1:7). This is in line with how Paul must have felt, when he said, "...I am compelled to preach. Woe to me if I do not preach the gospel!" (1 Cor.9:16). Jeremiah's "I am only a child"—excuse was surrounded by the Lord's absolute assurance, "Do not be afraid of them, for I am with you and will rescue you" (1:8).

Following the prohibition, commissioning and promise of protection, the Lord reached out his hand and touched Jeremiah's mouth and said to him, "Now I have put my words in your mouth. See, today I appoint you over nations and kingdoms to uproot and tear down, to destroy and overthrow, to build and to plant" (1:9-10). The touch of God on his mouth represents the personal nature of Jeremiah's calling. He acquired the message through an intimate act that symbolized purification (Isa.6:7).

This "hands-on" first-person dedication emphasized the de-constructive and constructive nature of God's message through Jeremiah. His work was tied exclusively to the Word of the Lord. It involved a painful "no" to ungodliness and a powerful "yes" to the will of God (Titus 2:12). It was far more important for Jeremiah to be faithful and submissive to the Word of the Lord than to be clever and inventive with his opinions. His work was not a medium for self-expression, but a holy vocation shaped by divine revelation. His mission belonged to God. It was imperative that he identify himself with God's will and purpose.

The Lord drew Jeremiah into his calling through a simple rebuke, a compelling purpose, positive assurance, and the gift of an unambiguous message. Then, as if that were not enough, the Lord caused Jeremiah to experience two visions. The vision of the blossoming almond tree, which was the first tree to bud in spring, was a sign of the immediate fulfillment of God's word. The second vision, that of the boiling pot tilting away from the north and pouring out disaster, signified that God would render judgment on Jerusalem by use of the Babylonian army. The visions enhance the vividness of Jeremiah's calling by igniting his praying imagination.

Jeremiah's orientation to God's work was emotionally and intellectually complete and his ordination to God's message was physically and spiritually compelling. Now all that was left to do was to finalize Jeremiah's commissioning with a summary charge, "Get yourself ready!"; a strong warning, "Do not be terrified by them or I will terrify you before them;"and a categorical promise, "I have made you a fortified city, an iron pillar and a bronze wall to stand against the whole land...for I am with you and will rescue you," declares the Lord" (1:17-19).

Two Weaknesses

It is important to distinguish between a weakness that begs for pity and a weakness that prays for strength. Weakness can foster a false dependency on others or a true dependency on God. Although it may seem harsh to say, it needs to be said that some people cling to their weakness as their own personal claim to significance, a merit badge inviting sympathy. It provides them with a convenient excuse for remaining as they are instead of a compelling reason for becoming what God calls them to be. A good church not only attracts people who are weak, broken, confused, and hurt, but offers Christ to heal their wounds, restore their souls and lead them in paths of righteousness. The Word of the Lord called Jeremiah out of a narrow life of his own making. A life that would have been mired in self-pity, self-reliance, feelings of inadequacy and insecurity. And the Word of the Lord called him into a great life, a bold life, filled with God's purpose and meaning. Jeremiah shows us what it means to take up our cross and follow the Lord Jesus Christ.

There are two kinds of weakness. There is the carnal weakness of the world that succumbs to sin and the sacrificial weakness of the cross that resists sin. One form of weakness must be overcome and the other must be embraced. The apostle Paul describes his attitude toward the latter, when he writes, "I will boast all the more gladly about my weaknesses, so that Christ's power may rest on me. That is why, for Christ's sake, I delight in weaknesses, in insults, in hardships, in persecutions, in difficulties. For when I am weak, then I am strong" (2 Cor.12:9-11). Religious types have a tendency to cling to worldly weakness and use grace as an excuse. They confuse faith in Christ with faith in themselves. They dwell on their weaknesses and make faith in Christ not about Christ and his grace, but about themselves and their effort.

This self-focus must be eliminated. In our own strength there is no hope of overcoming worldly weakness, but in Christ we are delivered from our pride and anxiety. We can embrace the weakness of the cross and depend upon his grace as an empowerment to obey

God's will. It is not about our heroic effort, but about what Christ has done for us and in us.

The church that entertains the admirers of Jesus and caters to their felt-needs inevitably attracts a host of self-absorbed weaklings who have no intention of changing their ego-centric ways. They use their many weaknesses to bully the church into paying attention to them. They are narcissistic, hungry for attention, eager to have their opinion heard and absorbed in their own story. Frequently they have left a trail of relational destruction in their path, but they have no intention of setting things right. When they attempt to serve others they are usually more trouble than they're worth, because they serve according to their whim and preference, always expecting to receive high praise for their efforts. Christ did not call his followers to this kind of weakness. This is the sin-nursing, blame-casting weakness that Christ came to overcome.

No one can read the Book of Jeremiah and honestly come up with the idea that its okay for the people of God to be slothful, complacent, fearful, permissive and indulgent. This is the bondage to sin that God seeks to liberate us from. We are no longer trapped in an endless cycle of good intentions, followed by sin and guilt, and another stab at good intentions. So when the apostle Paul says, "the Spirit helps us in our weakness," he does not mean that the Spirit is sympathetic to our carnal desires and condones our sin. He is not referring to the weakness due to our sin, but the weakness that comes from entering into solidarity with God and his redemptive purposes. This is the weakness that all creation feels as it waits for liberation from its bondage to decay. This is the weakness that groans inwardly "as we wait eagerly for our adoption, the redemption of our bodies" (Rom.8:23). This is the weakness that intercedes on behalf of others with the help of the Holy Spirit. This is the cross-bearing weakness that knows that nothing can separate us from the love of Christ. This is the weakness that knows we are more than conquerors through him who loved us, and knows this without any hint of pride. This new vulnerability is not the result of sin, but of obedience.

2. The Message

"This is what the Lord says: 'I
remember the devotion of your youth,
how as a bride you loved me . . . '"
Jeremiah 2:2

Like the movie previews we see in the theaters, this entire section (2:1-6:30) is made up of clips from various messages that Jeremiah delivered over decades of prophetic ministry. While the timing of the messages may range from Josiah's rule (627 BC) to the invasion of Nebuchadnezzar's army (587 BC), the place where these messages were delivered is firmly established in Jerusalem. We are reminded throughout the book that Jeremiah's calling was focused: "Go and proclaim in the hearing of Jerusalem" (2:1). In this section alone, Jerusalem is referred to fourteen times. Like Jesus who "resolutely set out for Jerusalem" (Luke 9:51), Jeremiah's ministry was centered in Jerusalem.

By the time we get to Jeremiah, Jerusalem has become ground zero in salvation history. In the days of Elijah and Elisha in the ninth century, and Hosea, Amos, and Jonah in the eighth century, the focus was on apostasy in the northern kingdom (Israel). Isaiah and Micah, contemporaries of Amos, focused on the southern kingdom (Judah), but it was left to Jeremiah in the seventh century to bring the message home to Jerusalem in the decades leading up to the exile. For forty years Jeremiah was stationed in a single spiritual war zone. He walked the same streets, saw the same people, and delivered the same message. Jeremiah lived an incredibly focused life. He was not only consecrated (1:5), his ministry focus was concentrated! It is notable that a ministry confined to a few square miles should have such a lasting and far reaching impact.

Jilted Lover

The message, like the call, was radically God-centered. Jeremiah began with a lament, but it was not his own, it was the Lord's lament charged with emotive metaphors and a stinging indictment. God, the jilted lover, the abandoned husband, was simply forgotten, in spite of the fact that at the outset Israel was a devoted bride and a recipient of God's Exodus power and Promised Land blessings. The prophets Hosea and Isaiah had used this marriage imagery to capture the Lord's love for his people (Isa.54:4-10; Hos.1-2) and the apostle Paul used it to describe Christ's love for the church (Eph.4:25). Throughout Salvation History the Lord has used the intimacy of marriage to illustrate the personal relationship and communion God offers us in Christ. The apostle John used "the wedding supper of the Lamb" to unite love and redemption in a personal relationship with the risen Lord Jesus Christ (Rev.19:7-9).

These two loves, marital love and divine love, romantic love and redemptive love, are meant to support and illuminate each other. The lesser love, the love between husband and wife, is meant to help us grasp more completely the personal intimacy and earnestness of God's love for us. The greater love, God's sacrificial, saving love, is meant to be the source, strength and standard for human love. The power and intensity of the oneness experienced between a man and a woman points to the greater mystery of our oneness with God in Christ.

The demise of Israel's devotion to God began more as a matter of default and neglect than outright denial and rebellion. They simply stopped inquiring of the Lord. "They did not ask, 'Where is the Lord, who brought us up out of Egypt and led us through the barren wilderness...'? ... "The priests did not ask, 'Where is the Lord?' The Lord was like the innocent party in a tragic marriage to a spouse who flaunted, first her indifference and then her infidelity. Israel's priests had become religious professionals instead of worship leaders, her teachers had become "scholars who knew everything but the Lord," her rulers ignored the rules, and her prophets equated Yahweh and Baal.[v]

It was wrong for pagan people to go after idols but a double tragedy for the professing people of God to exchange the glory of God for worthless idols (2:11; see Rom.1:23). It was bad enough for the northern kingdom of Israel to practice spiritual infidelity, but a double tragedy for Judah to ignore Israel's devastation and turn away from Yahweh (2:14-15; 3:6-11). The sobering message for those who profess faith in Christ today is that we, like Judah, may drift away from God's good news through complacency and indifference and turn to the popular idols of our day, self-worship, success, and sex. This is why the author of Hebrews said, "We must pay more careful attention, therefore, to what we have heard, so that we do not drift away" (Heb 2:1). This is why he contemplated the unthinkable: What would happen to believers who had tasted of the heavenly gift, shared in the Holy Spirit, and tasted the goodness of the Word of God, if they fell away (Heb.6:4-6)?

Jeremiah made the case against these professing believers, who were oblivious to their apostasy and yet serious about their religion, by using their own words to convict them. He had no shortage of evidence. He quoted their refusal to serve the Lord, "I will not serve you!" (2:20), and then gave verbatim their insistence on running after foreign gods, "It's no use! I love foreign gods, and I must go after them" (2:25). He quoted their devotional words to inanimate objects, "You are my father," and "You gave me birth" (2:27) and then cited their empty talk about Yahweh, "He will do nothing! No harm will come to us; we will never see sword or famine" (5:12). He recalled their prayers when they got into trouble, "Come and save us!" (2:27) and reminded them of their arrogance when they were trouble-free, "We are free to roam; we will come to you no more" (2:31). Their religious rhetoric could sound very pious, such as "My Father, my friend from my youth, will you always be angry? Will your wrath continue forever?", but then their actions were just as evil as ever (3:4-5). They liked saying, "As surely as the Lord lives," to cover up their lies (5:2).

Jeremiah made the case against these professing believers with rapid-fire images that visualized their zeal for spiritual apostasy. He likened their chasing after foreign gods to a donkey in heat or a roadside prostitute waiting to be picked up or an unfaithful wife (2:23; 3:2,20). He linked spiritual apostasy and sexual adultery together in such a way that disobedience in one area led inevitably to disobedience in the other area. From Jeremiah's perspective, idolatry and infidelity were inseparable. Jeremiah's tragic picture of Judah's home life included rebellious children, perverted sexuality and cheating spouses. His images speak volumes, "They are well-fed, lusty stallions, each neighing for another man's wife" (5:8). But the people are as oblivious to this tragedy as an old prostitute is to love (4:30). For Jeremiah, sexual immorality captured in a particularly poignant way the spiritual faithlessness of Judah. What should have been a beautiful marriage between God and his people was now nothing more than a sordid, scandalous situation.

But there was more to false spirituality than illicit sexuality and idolatry. Sexual promiscuity and economic oppression were linked not only in the mind of the prophet but in reality. "How skilled you are at pursuing [sex]! Even the worst of women can learn from your ways. On your clothes men find the lifeblood of the innocent poor, though you did not catch them breaking in" (2:33-34). Jeremiah likened the wicked to bird catchers, snatching people up and trapping them for their evil purposes. They live in houses full of deceit. They are healthy and sleek and their evil actions know no limit. "They do not plead the case of the fatherless *to win it*, they do not defend the rights of the poor" (5:28). This accusation leaves room for the wicked to appear to be on the side of the poor and orphaned when in fact they are not.

Mercy Judgment

There was only one conclusion to be drawn from all this evidence. "'Should I not punish them for this?'" declares the Lord. 'Should I not avenge myself on such a nation as this? A horrible and shocking thing has happened in the land: The prophets prophesy lies, the priests rule by their own authority, and my people love it this way. But what will you do in the end?" (5:29-31). To allow evil to go unchecked is evil itself. The evidence demanded a verdict that was both necessary and painful.

Jeremiah was tasked with not only making the case against his people, but describing the judgment to follow. "Announce in Judah and proclaim in Jerusalem and say: 'Sound the trumpet throughout the land! Cry aloud and say....Flee for safety without delay! For I am bringing disaster from the north, even terrible destruction'"(4:5-6). This was difficult for Jeremiah to do, because the people were totally unsuspecting of this message of judgment, in spite of the work of Habakkuk and Zephaniah. Jeremiah cried out, "Ah, Sovereign Lord, how completely you have deceived this people and Jerusalem by saying, 'You will have peace,' when the sword is at our throats" (4:10-12). Furthermore they had no shame. "Are they ashamed of their loathsome conduct?" the Lord asks rhetorically. "No, they have no shame at all," he answers, "they do not even know how to blush" (6:15). They were oblivious to the consequences of their evil actions and their complacency was reinforced by complicity of the leaders who minimized their sin. "They dress the wound of my people as though it were not serious," the Lord complained. "'Peace, peace,' they say, when there is no peace" (6:14). This made Jeremiah's ministry all the more necessary. He must not only pronounce the Lord's judgment against Jerusalem, but he must defend the justice of this punishment. Therefore he reminded them, "Your own conduct and actions have brought this upon you. This is your punishment. How bitter it is! How it pierces to the heart!" (4:18).

Against the people's complacency and the priests' complicity, Jeremiah was called to pronounce the Lord's comprehensive and catastrophic judgments against Judah (4:13-17, 23-29; 5:15-17; 6:1-9, 21-26). Jeremiah saw this judgment as so cataclysmic that creation reverted to its primeval state of chaos, "I looked at the earth, and it was formless and empty; at the heavens, and their light was gone. I looked at the mountains, and they were quaking; all the hills were swaying. I looked, and there were no people; every bird in the sky had flown away" (4:23-25). It would be an understatement to say that it was difficult for Jeremiah to prophesy this judgment. It was in fact a terrible burden that took a heavy toll on Jeremiah. It belies the myth that obedience to the will of God comes without suffering and grief. Jeremiah's anguish over delivering this message against his people and the Lord's anguish over having to punish his people appear to merge, so that at times it is difficult to know whether it is the Lord or Jeremiah speaking.

> "Oh, my anguish, my anguish!
> I writhe in pain.
> Oh, the agony of my heart!
> My heart pounds within me,
> I cannot keep silent.

For I have heard the sound of the trumpet;
I have heard the battle cry.
Disaster follows disaster;
the whole land lies in ruins.

In an instant my tents are destroyed,
my shelter in a moment.
How long must I see the battle standard
and hear the sound of the trumpet?
My people are fools;
they do not know me.
They are senseless children;
they have no understanding.
They are skilled in doing evil;
they know not how to do good."
(4:19-22; see 6:10-11)

We would find it easier and less convicting if Jeremiah's message could be limited to seventh century BC Judah, but the way in which the Lord Jesus drew from Jeremiah's teaching makes this restriction impossible. Jeremiah's critique reaches into our own time and challenges the church's propensity to forsake "the spring of living water" for "broken cisterns that cannot hold water" (2:13). As he did with the Samaritan woman at the well, Jesus offers us "living water," but we are tempted to dig our own wells that cannot provide water (John 4:10; see Rev.21:6). Judah's refusal to live under the yoke of obedience and service to God causes us to think of Jesus' invitation to his disciples, "Take my yoke upon you and learn from me, for I am gentle and humble in heart, and you will find rest for your souls. For my yoke is easy and my burden is light" (2:20; 5:5; Matt.11:29-30). Jeremiah likened Judah to a "corrupt, wild vine," an image Jesus used when he said, "I am the vine; you are the branches. If you remain in me and I in you, you will bear much fruit; apart from me you can do nothing. If you do not remain in me, you are like a branch that is thrown away and withers; such branches are picked up, thrown into the fire and burned" (John 15:5-6; see Jer. 2:21). The obvious affinity that Jesus had for Jeremiah's message underscores its significance for his disciples today.

Return to Me

Redemption, not condemnation, was at the heart of Jeremiah's message. At the center of this spiraling whirlwind of judgment was a message of hope. The eye of the storm was calm. There were flashes of light and hope penetrating an otherwise dark and doomed situation. Jeremiah issued the Lord's impassioned appeal to return to him. He began with the northern kingdom of Israel (3:11-12), a sign that the message of hope extended to all those who were lost, and emphasized the Lord's mercy (3:12), election (3:14), filial faithfulness (3:19), healing (3:22), and blessing (4:2). As a sign of the sincerity and comprehensiveness of the appeal, the Lord's "Return to me" message was repeated four times (3:12, 14, 22; 4:1). It is also an indication that Jeremiah gave this message repeatedly. It was a message of renewal based on God's mercy and his desire to be intimate with his people. "'Return, faithless people,' declares the Lord, 'for I am your husband'" (3:14). In spite of their faithlessness and the "stubbornness of their evil hearts" (3:17) God was eager to treat them as family and give them an inheritance.

Consider the pathos behind the line, "I thought you would call me 'Father' and not turn away from following me" (3:19). In the midst of an intentionally intimidating message of judgment, Jeremiah expressed God's longing for an intimate relationship with his people. His prophecy anticipates "the Spirit of sonship" whereby "we cry, 'Abba, Father,'" because "the Spirit testifies with our spirit that we are God's children" (Rom.8:15-16).

Jeremiah's message of hope looks forward to a new day when Zion will be home to God's elect. True shepherds with a heart for God, instead of greedy, dysfunctional leaders (2:8; 5:31; 6:13-14), will lead the people "with knowledge and understanding" (3:15). Jeremiah's Spirit-inspired vision of a New Covenant, renders the old covenant with its ark and ethnic privilege obsolete, because all the nations will gather around the throne of the Lord in Jerusalem (3:16-18). Jeremiah anticipates that day when "at the name of Jesus every knee should bow, in heaven and on earth and under the earth, and every tongue confess that Jesus Christ is Lord, to the glory of God the Father" (Phil.2:10).

Having explored the reasons and motivation for returning to the Lord, Jeremiah explained *how* to return. In contrast to his anguished description of the complexities of evil, Jeremiah offered a simple way home to the Lord, "Only acknowledge your guilt—you have rebelled against the Lord your God..." (3:13). He even went so far as to give them the words to say. He wrote out their confession for them. In effect he led them in prayer, saying,

> "Yes, we will come to you,
> for you are the Lord our God.

Surely the idolatrous commotion
on the hills and mountains is a deception;
surely in the Lord our God
is the salvation of Israel.
From our youth shameful gods have
consumed the fruits of our fathers'
labor–their flocks and herds,
their sons and daughters.
Let us lie down in our shame,
and let our disgrace cover us.
We have sinned against the Lord our God,
both we and our fathers;
from our youth till this day
we have not obeyed the Lord our God."
(3:22-25).

For the people confronted by Jeremiah, repentance
was a foreign concept, but that was no excuse for not
delivering the Lord's message. Their complex strategies of
self-deception and a long history of resistance to
repentance made it doubly hard, but Jeremiah persisted. He
declared what the Lord wanted him to say, "Break up your
unplowed ground and do not sow among thorns.
Circumcise yourselves to the Lord, circumcise your
hearts..." (4:3-4). The agricultural metaphors of unplowed
ground and thorns bring to mind Jesus' parable of the
sower and the soils (Mark 4:1-20; Matt.13:1-23; Luke 8:1-
15). Jeremiah was working in a tough field. The people
were really into religious rituals like circumcision, but these
rituals had long since ceased to symbolize true faith in
Yahweh and obedience to his word. Nevertheless Jeremiah
was called to be bold and to minister with undaunted
courage. The Lord promised, "I will make my words in

your mouth a fire and these people the wood it consumes" (5:14). On another occasion the Lord used a telling image to describe Jeremiah and to visualize the people's resistance to his ministry. The Lord said, "I have made you a tester of metals and my people the ore, that you may observe and test their ways. They are all hardened rebels, going about to slander. They are bronze and iron; they all act corruptly. The bellows blow fiercely to burn away the lead with fire, but the refining goes on in vain; the wicked are not purged out. They are called rejected silver, because the Lord has rejected them" (6:27-30).

Jeremiah's message brings the disciples of the Lord Jesus Christ to the crossroads. We stand at the intersection of a true passion for Christ and a life-deadening religion-as-usual. Every era faces the tragic temptation to reduce God to a jilted lover, an abandoned spouse, whose redemptive love is spurned with either cold-shoulder neglect or out-right contempt. We remember how seriously the Lord treated the church at Ephesus. Although they performed good deeds, they had lost their first love. We need to hear the warning that they heard, "Remember the height from which you have fallen! Repent and do the things you did at first" (Rev.2:5). We don't want our devotion to God to a be but a forgotten memory as it was for Judah (2:2), but instead we want it to be a living, vital relationship that grows and deepens as we learn to trust and obey our risen Lord. Jeremiah's prophecy confronts us with a choice: "Stand at the crossroads and look; ask for the ancient paths, ask where the good way is, and walk in it, and you will find rest for your souls" (6:16). As the Lord's prophet, Jeremiah's "Return-to-me" message remains effective preparation for

Jesus' "Come-to-me" message, because there is only one source for true rest and love. "Come to me," Jesus said, "all you who are weary and burdened, and I will give you rest. Take my yoke upon you and learn from me, for I am gentle and humble in heart, and you will find rest for your souls. For my yoke is easy and my burden is light" (Matt.11:28-30).

3. The Prophet in the House

*"Do not trust in deceptive words
and say, 'This is the temple of the
Lord, the temple of the Lord, the
temple of the Lord!'"* Jeremiah 7:4

This section is framed by Jeremiah's presence in the Jerusalem temple. It begins with his temple address which took place shortly after Jehoiakim came to power in 609 BC (7:1; see 26:1) and ends with Pashhur, the chief officer of the temple, ordering Jeremiah to be beaten and placed in the stocks (20:1-2). The material bracketed by these two events covers a range of tough issues: social injustice, flagrant idolatry, spiritual arrogance, and moral indifference. Woven into the fabric of this prophetic critique of contemporary spirituality is Jeremiah's own pain and grief. "Since my people are crushed, I am crushed; I mourn, and horror grips me" (8:21-22).

Jeremiah was positioned strategically to deliver the Word of the Lord. His message stands as a striking antithesis to everything that popular religion stood for, both then and now. He attacked the spiritual complacency, religious pluralism, idolatry, immorality and ethical relativism of his day with such clarity and boldness that the meaning of his message was never in doubt. In our own age of equivocation and compromise, Jeremiah stands as a powerful reminder of Jesus' confrontation with the religious leaders of his day, as well as a painful reminder of the price that can be paid for standing true to the Word of God.

Jeremiah had no official authority nor professional credentials other than his God-given responsibility to deliver the Word of the Lord. He held no position of leadership nor represented any recognizable constituency. He was neither famous nor entertaining. He was not the kind of speaker one invited to fund-raising banquets, prayer breakfasts and college commencements. He had no institutional platform from which to promote his message and no advance team to set the stage for his work. But we would be mistaken if we think of Jeremiah as some fly-by-night, self-styled, self-proclaimed prophet, like the homeless street preacher who loves to shout on street corners.

Before Jeremiah stood at the entrance of the temple he stood in a long tradition of prophets who had been created, called, consecrated and commissioned by the Lord God. As we have seen, he assumed his God-given responsibility reluctantly. Far from being a high-energy, egocentric extrovert who fed off of the energy of the crowd, Jeremiah strikes us as a quiet, thoughtful man, who cared deeply for the Lord and his people.

Jeremiah stood where God told him to stand, "Stand at the gate of the Lord's house and there proclaim this message..." (7:2). If Jerusalem was ground zero, then the temple was the epicenter. It was there that Jeremiah proclaimed, "Hear the Word of the Lord, all you people of

Judah who come through these gates to worship the Lord.
This is what the Lord Almighty, the God of Israel, says..."
(7:2-3). Jeremiah was not sent to sit down and try to
negotiate a compromise nor arbitrate between conflicting
opinions. He was called to stand up and proclaim a clear,
unambiguous, nonnegotiable message from the Lord. If his
message had been inspired by his plan for Judah, then he
should have negotiated with the people. If his vision had
been a reflection of his personality and based on his wish
dreams then he should have been open to incorporating
other people's opinions and perspectives. But Jeremiah's
message was not his by right of authorship or invention, but
his by way of obedience and faithfulness to the Word of the
Lord. Therefore, it was impossible for Jeremiah to be over-
bold, too intense or overly dogmatic with the message he
was called to proclaim. His proclamation involved
explanation, not negotiation. He gave assertions, not
suggestions; orders, not options. He delivered the Lord's
ultimatums, not his personal opinions.

Martin Luther reflected the spirit of the prophet
Jeremiah when he said to Erasmus, "To take no pleasure in
assertions is not the mark of a Christian heart; indeed, one
must delight in assertions to be a Christian at all." "By
'assertion,' Luther explained, "I mean staunchly holding your
ground, stating your position, confessing it, defending it and
persevering in it unvanquished. I do not think that the term
has any other meaning...[Of course] I am talking about the
assertion of what has been delivered to us from above in the
Sacred Scriptures."vi It was because the Lord told Jeremiah
to "stand up" and say whatever he commanded him to say,
that he was made like "a fortified city, an iron pillar and a
bronze wall to stand against the whole land" (1:18).

Popular Spirituality

Some pastors measure courage by promoting a building campaign or switching from traditional worship music to contemporary music, but not Jeremiah. It must have taken real courage for Jeremiah to stand at the gate of the temple and say, "This is what the Lord Almighty, the God of Israel says: Reform your ways and your actions, and I will let you live in this place. Do not trust in deceptive words and say, 'This is the temple of the Lord, the temple of the Lord, the temple of the Lord!'" (7:3-4). Jeremiah drew a bold distinction between the authoritative Word of the Lord and the deceptive words, "the temple of the Lord, the temple of the Lord, the temple of the Lord." Most of the people the prophet faced would have equated the temple of the Lord with the Word of the Lord, but not Jeremiah. He saw a critical difference between heartfelt righteousness and religious enthusiasm. As Eugene Peterson says, "The church is never in so much danger as when it is popular and millions of people are saying 'I'm born again, born again, born again.'"[vii]

In Jeremiah's day, ritual practices were well attended. The temple liturgy was lively. Priests were popular. Religious diversity was culturally inclusive, meaning that both Baal and Yahweh were highly respected. Sincerity was what counted the most. Lay people talked about their faith journeys and scribes discussed the law of the Lord. Expensive sacrifices were presented with fanfare. But evidence of basic obedience was absent, foreigners were oppressed, the fatherless were abused, widows were isolated, and the poor were exploited. Idolatry was widespread, along with violence and moral decadence. Jeremiah posed Yahweh's question, "Will you steal and murder, commit adultery and perjury, burn incense to Baal and follow other gods you have not known, and then come and stand before me in this house, which bears my Name, and say, 'We are safe'—safe to do all these detestable things? Has this house, which bears my Name, become a den of robbers to you?" (7:9-11). The long tradition of respect for the house of the Lord (2 Sam.7:12-13; Ps.132:13-14) was pretentiously maintained while despising everything the Name of the Lord stood for.

Worse than no religion at all is a religion reduced to self-expression, self-gratification, and self-indulgence. When Marx condemned institutional religion as the opiate of the people, he was close to the truth. And there is undoubtedly some truth behind Freud's dismissal of sentimental religion based on the childish illusion of the need for a father figure. It is not surprising that astrophysicist Carl Sagan concluded that religion was a superstition modern science would eventually destroy. Nor is it surprising that the demise of religion as it is popularly conceived and practiced has the Lord's endorsement. The difference between Jeremiah and the 20th century's leading de-bunkers of religion is that the prophet distinguished between an authentic relationship with the Lord God and they didn't. For them all religion was bad, but for Jeremiah that would be like saying all marriage is bad because there are adulterers or that all families are bad because some parents abuse their children.

How bad was Judah's temple religion? Jeremiah painted a vivid picture of blatant idolatry, false sacrifices, and deceptive leaders. Idolatry was a family affair. "The children gather wood, the fathers light the fire, and the women knead the dough and make cakes of bread for the Queen of Heaven" (7:18). Scholars identify the Queen of Heaven with the Assyro-Babylonian goddess Ishtar. Burning incense and pouring out drink offerings to this maternal figure was thought to assure material well-being (44:17-19). Is the Spirit of Sport or the Cult of Self-Esteem modern equivalents to the Queen of Heaven? Do families today neglect the worship of God because they are engrossed in sports? Do well-meaning people ignore the living God and cater to their own welfare? Has popular religion attempted to justify, in the name of "family values," the devotion of our time, energy and resources to pursuits that compete with our devotion to God? Undoubtedly the people in Jeremiah's day felt it was an innocent and beneficial exercise to pay respect to the gods of other cultures. But it was not an innocent exercise, because it provoked the Lord. It would be sad if what the Lord said of them could be said of us, "Are they not rather harming themselves, to their own shame?"(7:19).

In spite of all the lavish and artistic attention offered to idols, Jeremiah contended that they were nothing more than silent scarecrows in a melon patch (10:5). He contrasted idols with "the living God, the eternal King," who "made the earth by his power," "the world by his wisdom, and stretched out the heavens by his understanding" (10:10, 12). The prophet asserted that the sin-twisted inclination to turn inanimate objects into symbols of virility, success, and pleasure, made no sense at all. Today's secularized culture has infused spiritual value in such things as cars and homes and human bodies. We do not worship biological fertility but we worship material success and sexual pleasure. Nor did the sacrifices paid to idols produce anything positive. In Jeremiah's day there was no shortage of ritual sacrifices. People were eager to sacrifice liberally both to Yahweh and to the pagan gods. They followed a *whatever* philosophy of religion that sought to appease all the gods, and the Lord was not pleased. "Go ahead," declared the Lord, "add your burnt offerings to your other sacrifices and eat the meat yourselves!" (7:21).

The most extreme form of false sacrifice cost the lives of their children. Jeremiah referred to the infamous Valley of Ben Hinnom, which eventually became Jerusalem's refuse dump and "whose shortened name *gehenna* meets us in the New Testament's word for hell."[viii] It was there that King Manasseh began the detestable practice of human sacrifice (2 Kings 23:10). The twisted religious rationale for this may have come from the Ammonites who sacrificed their children to appease the pagan deity Molech. It is argued that some religious leaders may have reasoned that this is what Yahweh wanted when he called for the dedication of all first-born (Ex.13:2; see Mic.6:7).[ix] This may explain why the Lord condemned this practice as "something I did not command nor did it enter my mind" (7:31; 19:5). It is hard to fathom the tragedy of people sacrificing their children to appease the gods, until one realizes that people today regularly sacrifice their children to pursue their own selfish ends. They don't burn them on a literal altar, but they neglect or abandon or spoil them. A strong case can be made that moderns, like the ancients, put their children on a sacrificial altar, not for the sake of a pagan deity, but for the sake of pagan desires.

Taking a Stand

When Jeremiah stood at the gate of the temple to proclaim the Lord's message against blatant idolatry and false sacrifice, he took his stand in a long tradition that valued obedience over ritual and humble devotion over religious performance. He stood with Abel and his sacrificial lamb, against Cain's offering of choice produce (Gen. 4). He stood with Moses, who climbed down Mount Sinai to oppose Aaron's Golden Calf Festival to the Lord (Ex. 32).

He stood with faithful Samuel against Saul's religion of convenience (1 Sam.13). He stood with a repentant King David when he prayed, "You do not delight in sacrifice, or I would bring it; you do not take pleasure in burnt offerings. The sacrifices of God are a broken spirit; a broken and contrite heart, O God, you will not despise" (Ps.51:16-17). He stood with Amos, who declared the Word of the Lord, "I hate, I despise your religious feasts; I cannot stand your assemblies. Even though you bring me burnt offerings and grain offerings, I will not accept them....But let justice roll on like a river, righteousness like a never-failing stream!" (Amos 5:21-24). He stood in the tradition of Hosea, who spoke for God when he said, "For I desire mercy, not sacrifice, and acknowledgment of God rather than burnt offerings" (Hos.6:6). He stood with Micah, when the prophet contrasted hyper religiosity with simple obedience, saying, "He has showed you, O man, what is good. And what does the Lord require of you? To act justly and to love mercy and to walk humbly with your God" (Mic.6:8). He stood with the prophet Isaiah when he said hear the Word of the Lord, "Stop bringing meaningless offerings! Your incense is detestable to me....I cannot bear your evil assemblies...Stop doing wrong, learn to do right! Seek justice, encourage the oppressed. Defend the cause of the fatherless, plead the case of the widow" (Isa.1:13-17).

Jeremiah kept this long tradition going, but his most important connection was not to the past but to the future, not to the prophets he echoed but to the Savior he preceded. Standing at the gate of the Lord's house, he leveled a blistering attack against those who took comfort in their outward performance and religious ritual. On behalf of the Lord he asked, "Has this house, which bears my Name, become a den of robbers to you?" (7:11). This stinging accusation recalls Jesus at the temple, when he forcibly drove out "all who were buying and selling" and "overturned the tables of the money changers." "It is written," Jesus said, quoting the prophet Isaiah, "'My house will be called a house of prayer,' but you are making it a *den of robbers.*'"(Matt.21:13; see Isa.56:7; Jer.7:11). By drawing on both Isaiah and Jeremiah, Jesus equated the religious crisis of his day with the false temple religion that the prophets had confronted. His words and actions vindicated the work of the prophets through the centuries as they sought to drive out empty religiosity, meaningless ritual and self-righteousness. The prophet Habakkuk's imperative is timely, "The Lord is in his holy temple; let all the earth be silent before him" (Hab.2:20).

The Lord Declares War

Just as Jesus confronted the scribes and Pharisees and teachers of the law, Jeremiah confronted the leaders of his day. Jeremiah attributed the people's ignorance of "the requirements of the Lord" to the distorted theology and ethical malpractice of the priests, prophets, scribes, and officials (8:8). These religious professionals handled the law but did not know the Lord nor the law. They did not ask, "Where is the Lord?" and they were unable and unwilling to make the simple distinction between Yahweh and Baal (2:8). Judah's leaders were like disgraced executives (2:26) with their greedy selfishness exposed and their deceitfulness uncovered (6:13). They were like lackadaisical physicians, telling patients with life-threatening diseases to go home and take an aspirin. The Lord complained, "They dress the wound of my people as though it were not serious. 'Peace, peace,' they say, when there is no peace'" (6:14).

It would have been better if the priests and scribes had rejected the law of God altogether, but instead they proudly laid claim to the Bible before proceeding to twist and distort its message. "'How can you say,' Jeremiah asked, 'We are wise, for we have the law of the Lord, when actually the lying pen of the scribes has handled it falsely?'" This is a grave problem today, because many of our so-called professional biblical scholars attribute more integrity and authenticity to Shakespeare's writings than they do to Scripture. They revere the U.S. Constitution with more awe and appreciation than they do the four Gospels. Many modern day biblical scholars read the Bible as a collection of diverse religious experiences. They do not read it as the sure Word of God. Both then and now, when "the shepherds are senseless and do not inquire of the Lord, they do not prosper and all their flock is scattered" (10:21). As Jeremiah concluded, "Since they have rejected the Word of the Lord, what kind of wisdom do they have?" (8:9). The answer to that question didn't need to be spelled out, but Jeremiah repeated what must have been the message of the times, "They dress the wound of my people as though it were not serious. 'Peace, peace,' they say, when there is no peace'" (8:11). It was against these leaders that the Lord called Jeremiah to declare war and deliver this verdict, "'So they will fall among the fallen; they will be brought down when they are punished,' says the Lord" (8:12).

Jeremiah was not competitive or pretentious. He provided a dramatically different model of leadership. In contrast to the spiritual indifference, professional demeanor, and religious enthusiasm of Judah's leaders, Jeremiah was filled with anguish and sorrow. Instead of a casual attitude and feel-good sermons, Jeremiah lamented the tragic state of his people. He cried out to God, "O, my Comforter in sorrow, my heart is faint within me...Since my people are crushed, I am crushed; I mourn, and horror grips me" (8:18-19, 21). He could not imagine why the people acted as if the Lord was no longer in Zion or why they refused to turn to him for healing. Why would you turn to idols when you could worship the living God? Implicit in Jeremiah's question, "Is there no balm in Gilead?" (a balsam wood resin that was used for medicinal purposes), is the obvious answer, Yes, of course there is. "Is there no physician there? Why then is there no healing for the wound of my people?" (8:22).

Jeremiah lamented the tragedy of it all, "Oh, that my head were a spring of water and my eyes a fountain of tears! I would weep day and night for the slain of my people" (9:1). He longed to get away from his responsibilities and his pain. He expressed his feelings openly, "At times I wish I had a wilderness hut, a backwoods cabin, where I could get away from my people and never see them again. They're a faithless, feckless bunch, a congregation of degenerates" (9:2; The Message). But Jeremiah stayed right where the Lord told him to stand. He never strayed from the Lord's will. He may have been overwhelmed with anguish, but even more importantly he was humbled before God. As he confronted those who were "stubborn" and "uncircumcised in heart" (9:14, 26), he became more sensitive to his own sin and his need for God's mercy. He prayed, "I know, O Lord, that a person's life is not his own; it is not for mortals to direct their steps. Correct me, Lord, but only with justice—not in your anger, lest you reduce me to nothing" (10:23-24). He followed in his own life the counsel the Lord gave him to give to others:

> "'Let not the wise man boast of his wisdom or
> the strong man boast of his strength or the rich

man boast of his riches, but let him who boasts boast about this; that he understands and knows me, that I am the Lord, who exercises kindness, justice and righteousness on earth, for in these I delight,' declares the Lord" (9:23-24).

Horror Scenes

Throughout his temple sermon Jeremiah reiterated the Lord's message of judgment. He sought to impress upon the people the grave consequences for their devotion to idols, deceptive leaders and false sacrifices, as well as their practice of social injustice, greed and violence. The invitation to revisit Shiloh provided historical evidence that God was serious about removing those who despised his name (7:12-15; see 1 Sam.1-4). God's intention was also evident in Jeremiah's description of the scope and intensity of judgment: "Therefore this is what the Sovereign Lord says: 'My anger and my wrath will be poured out on this place, on man and beast, on the trees of the field and on the fruit of the ground, and it will burn and not be quenched'" (7:20). Prophesying that the Valley of Ben Hinnom would become a killing field and that the graves of Jerusalem would be unearthed conveyed the extent of the devastation (7:32-8:3). In words reminiscent of Habakkuk, Jeremiah pronounced the Lord's judgment, "I will take away their harvest. There will be no grapes on the vine. There will be no figs on the tree, and their leaves will wither" (8:13; see Hab.3:17).

Today we try hard to make people feel good, but Jeremiah worked hard to help people visualize the consequences of their actions. He must have raised his voice when he said, "Cut off your hair and throw it away; take up a lament on the barren heights, for the Lord has rejected and abandoned this generation that is under his wrath" (7:29).

He pictured Jerusalem as "a heap of ruins, a haunt of jackals" where no one was safe anywhere, not even in one's bedroom. "Death has climbed in through our windows and has entered our fortresses; it has cut off the children from the streets and the young men from the public squares" (9:11, 21).

In addition to conveying the extent and the experience of the Lord's judgment, Jeremiah was impressed by its inevitability. It was impossible for the living God, who is holy and just, to ignore Judah's flagrant disobedience and willful rebellion. "'Should I not punish them for this?' declares the Lord. 'Should I not avenge myself on such a nation as this?'(5:29; 9:9). The answer was as obvious as it was devastating. For Jeremiah, the inevitability of judgment took on a particularly personal dimension. He was told three times not to pray for "this people." The first time the Lord said, "do not plead with me, for I will not listen to you" (7:16). The second time the Lord said, "Do not pray....because I will not listen when they call to me in the time of distress" (11:14). And the third time the Lord said, "Do not pray for the well-being of this people. Although they fast, I will not listen to their cry; though they offer burnt offerings and grain offerings, I will not accept them. Instead, I will destroy them with the sword, famine and plague" (14:11).

There are several important facts to keep in mind about this divine prohibition:

(1) Jeremiah came at the end of a long line of prophets who had been called to announce judgment against Judah. There had been plenty of opportunities for repentance and now the long-delayed moment of reckoning had finally come.

(2) The Lord was not about to assume the burden of responsibility that belonged to a people who had squandered every opportunity to return to him. Any attempt to "spiritualize" the judgment of God was to be rejected. Prayer must not be used to soften the message.

(3) The prohibition fit with the providence of God who knew the heart and mind of the people.

(4) Jeremiah was prohibited from praying for the welfare of "this people" but he was not prohibited from admonishing the people to repent and return to the Lord.

(5) Jeremiah was issued this personal prohibition personally for that particular time and it is not meant to be an excuse for us to reject praying for others.

Some sensitive people may take this message to heart and begin to think that they can never be forgiven by God and escape the final judgment. They feel it is too late for them to be prayed for and too late for them to pray. They may believe that their spiritual condition is beyond the grace of God and they have committed "the unforgivable sin." In the light of Jesus' warning, they may fear that they have sinned against the Holy Spirit: "Anyone who speaks a word against the Son of Man will be forgiven, but anyone who speaks against the Holy Spirit will not be forgiven, either in this age or in the age to come" (Matt.12:32). But this is to twist the meaning of Jeremiah's prohibition and Jesus' warning, because both statements were intended to encourage repentance and compel conversion.

Imagine the people's reaction when Jeremiah said in effect, "The Lord has told me to stop wasting my time praying for you." Such a statement should promote action not indifference and shock people out of their spiritual resistance. Likewise, with Jesus' warning, which roughly paraphrased meant, "Say what you want about me, but if you refuse the witness of the Holy Spirit you are doomed." The "unforgivable sin" was not some secret sin that a person may have unwittingly committed, but the persistent rejection of the Spirit's testimony about Jesus and that person's refusal to the bitter end of life to come to Christ for salvation. The intent of both Jeremiah's prohibition and Jesus' warning was the same: "Today, if you hear his voice, do not harden your hearts..." (Heb.3:15). Jesus told his followers, "Love your enemies and pray for those who persecute you, that you may be sons of your Father in heaven" (Matt.5:44). The greatest example of that imperative came on the Cross, when Jesus prayed, "Father, forgive them, for they do not know what they are doing" (Luke 23:34). There is no greater expression of God's readiness to forgive than the very words of the Savior from the Cross. There is no excuse for not turning to God.

4. Praying Our Pain

*"O Lord, you deceived me, and I was deceived; you
overpowered me and prevailed. I am ridiculed all day
long; everyone mocks me. Whenever I speak, I cry out
proclaiming violence and destruction. So the Word of
the Lord has brought me insult and reproach all day
long."* Jeremiah 20:7-8

Jeremiah was unrelenting in proclaiming the message of
judgment before the people of Jerusalem. He remained
undaunted and steadfast, refusing to cower to psychological
intimidation, betrayals, conspiracies, physical persecution,
imprisonment, and constant death threats. He delivered the
message of judgment in a variety of imaginative and
compelling ways. Through reasoned discourse from the
book of Deuteronomy he confronted the people with their
violation of the terms of the covenant (11:1-8). He attacked
the pride of Judah with simple, dramatic object lessons so
that no one could miss the message. His parables of
judgment included burying a linen belt (13:1-11), picturing
smashed wineskins (13:12-14), observing a potter rework his
clay (18:1-12), smashing a clay pot (19:1-13), using two
baskets of figs—one good the other rotten (24:2), and even
wearing a yoke around his neck (27:2).

To shape the context of Jeremiah's preaching the Lord God provided his own object lessons of judgment. He sent a drought which caused the people to mourn, but they mourned because of the drought, not their disobedience. "The nobles send their servants for water; they go to the cisterns but find no water. They return with their jars unfilled; dismayed and despairing, they cover their heads" (14:3). To intensify the impact of the message, the Lord directed Jeremiah to specific locations. Besides standing at the temple gate to deliver his message, Jeremiah was also sent to the potter's house and to the notorious Valley of Ben Hinnom where "the blood of the innocent" continued to be sacrificed (19:4-5).

Jeremiah's more dramatic messages were balanced with his straightforward, practical messages of reform, such as his call to keep the Sabbath holy (17:19-27). No one could accuse Jeremiah of being too abstract or theoretical. He brought the message home in powerful ways that the people could reject, but not ignore. Moreover, Jeremiah pictured the message of God so well that he himself became like a parable constantly pointing to the will of God. He not only *stood* for the message that he proclaimed, he also embodied it. The message shaped his personality, dictated his actions, governed his investments and endangered his life. The Word of the Lord shaped the medium, Jeremiah's life, and the medium became one with the message.

This was especially evident in Jeremiah's personal life. "The Word of the Lord came to me," reported Jeremiah, and said, "'You must not marry and have sons or daughters in this place" (16:2). By denying Jeremiah the joys of marriage and family life, the Lord pictured in the life of his prophet the future sorrow of Judah. By prohibiting Jeremiah from attending funerals and weddings, the Lord illustrated the coming desolation of his people. Jeremiah pictured what the Lord meant when he said, "I have withdrawn my blessing, my love and pity from this people....I will bring an end to the sounds of joy and gladness and to the voices of the bride and bridegroom in this place" (16:5, 9).

In public Jeremiah's message was "like a hammer that breaks a rock in pieces" (23:29), "like a burning fire, shut up in [his] bones," which he was unable to hold in (20:9). There was no hint of weakness in Jeremiah's public ministry, but in private, when he was alone with the Lord, he cried out to God in frustration and desperation. He complained bitterly about his enemies and lamented passionately about his life. His prayers run the gamut of emotions from blistering anger and raw hate to utter helplessness and overwhelming feelings of rejection. Throughout this section of the book, and only in this section, there is a threefold pattern of intensity. The initial factor involved Jeremiah's delivery of an intense message of judgment, often followed by life-threatening persecution. Then against this opposition Jeremiah responded with anguished prayers of lament that ranged from desperate cries for help to scandalous imprecations against his enemies. The third factor in this confessional paradigm was God's response to Jeremiah, which consistently refused to indulge his self-pity and challenged him to remain strong.

Praying our Frustration (12:1-4)

Jeremiah's prayers are a rare, behind-the-scenes, look at the inner life of a person working on the front-lines of a spiritual war zone. This section begins with his acute awareness of his personal vulnerability (11:18-23). The men from his hometown of Anathoth issued an ultimatum, saying, "Do not prophesy in the name of the Lord or you will die by our hands" (11:21). Up until now, we have no record of Jeremiah coming under fire personally. The people had condemned the Lord and rejected his word but there was no significant backlash against Jeremiah. But that all changed when men of Anathoth secretly plotted against him, saying, "Let us destroy the tree and its fruit; let us cut him off from the land of the living, that his name be remembered no more" (11:19).

Jeremiah was not looking for a fight and he certainly did not relish making people angry with him—angry enough to want to kill him. He admitted that he was naive about their animosity and unsuspecting of their threats. He likened himself to "a gentle lamb led to the slaughter" (11:19). Then as now, those who stand by the Word of the Lord will suffer persecution. Jesus prepared his followers for what to expect when they acknowledged him publicly. He said,

> "Do not suppose that I have come to bring peace to the earth. I did not come to bring peace, but a sword. For I have come to turn 'a man against his father, a daughter against her mother, a daughter-in-law against her mother-in-law—your enemies will be members of your own household'" (Matt.10:35).

What was happening to Jeremiah was what the Lord said in the Sermon on the Mount would happen to us,

> "Blessed are you when people insult you, persecute you and falsely say all kinds of evil against you because of me. Rejoice and be glad, because great is your reward in heaven, for in

the same way they persecuted the prophets who
were before you" (Matt.5:11-12).

Jeremiah's reaction to these harsh circumstances was to pray.
Instead of whining or debating or gossiping, he prayed real
prayers to the living God, not nicely worded ritualistic
prayers, but bold, straight-from-the-heart prayers. Prayer
makes perfect sense, especially when you know that the
living God created, called, consecrated and commissioned
you (1:4). Jeremiah's first line of defense against the terror
that confronted him was not to talk about God but to talk to
God. This simple spiritual discipline spared Jeremiah the
common mistake that many sincere believers make when
their naiveté is shattered and their vulnerability is exposed.
Instead of going to God they either talk to themselves and
carry on an inner monologue which feeds off their anxiety
and insecurity or they wear others out with their complaint.
Jeremiah was desperately frustrated, but instead of turning
inward or trying to escape the pain, he turned to God.

Like the faithful before him, Jeremiah prayed out his
frustration (see Ps.73; Job 21). He began,

> "You are always righteous, O Lord, when I
> bring a case before you. Yet I would speak with
> you about your justice: Why does the way of
> the wicked prosper? Why do all the faithless
> live at ease? You have planted them, and they
> have taken root; they grow and bear fruit. You
> are always on their lips but far from their
> hearts." (12:1-3).

His confession reflects an acute sense of moral pain,
intensified by the failure of his ministry to change hearts and

lives. Jeremiah felt what Søren Kierkegaard expressed, "Everything goes on as usual, and yet there is no longer anyone who believes in it." A thin veneer of religion-as-usual covered up strategies of deception and oppression that promoted the prosperity of the wicked. Yet the Lord seemed to condone the behavior of the faithless by permitting their comfort and success. "Meanwhile," Jeremiah complained, "you know *me* inside and out. You don't let me get by with a thing!" (12:3; The Message). The frustration of it all infuriated Jeremiah and ignited his hate. "Drag them off like sheep to be butchered!" he cried. "Set them apart for the day of slaughter!" Undoubtedly this metaphor occurred to him, because he felt "like a gentle lamb led to the slaughter" (11:19). Instead of the Lord being in control of the situation, Jeremiah felt like the people who were plotting his demise were in control, and they were saying in effect, "Jeremiah won't be around for long. He will not see what happens to us."

Jeremiah's personal vulnerability triggered this disturbing confession of hate. Like a wounded animal he had been backed into a corner and he came out praying. "Prayer is combat. Prayer brings us before God—and there, before God, we find ourselves grappling with "the world rulers of this present darkness, against the spiritual hosts of wickedness in the heavenly places" (Eph.6:12).[x] It is better to pray out our hate to God than act out our hate against others. "...Our hate needs to be prayed, not suppressed...Embarrassed by the ugliness and fearful of the murderous, we commonly neither admit or pray our hate; we deny it and suppress it. But if it is not admitted it can quickly and easily metamorphose into the evil that provokes it..."[xi] In his frustration, Jeremiah did three things right. Instead of turning away from God or talking about God, he talked to

God. Then, instead of acting out his hate, he prayed out his hate to God. And thirdly, he listened to what God had to say. The Lord wants us to pray boldly and speak our mind, but then we need to be open to hear what he has to say in his Word.

The Lord's answer to Jeremiah's feeling of vulnerability reminds us of his response to Job when the Lord said, "Who is this that darkens my counsel with words without knowledge? Brace yourself like a man; I will question you, and you shall answer me" (Job 38:2-3). The Lord did not give Jeremiah soothing answers or a pat on the back, he challenged him, saying, "If you have raced with men on foot and they have worn you out, how can you compete with horses? If you stumble in safe country, how will you manage in the thickets by the Jordan?" The Lord said to Jeremiah in effect, "Face the facts. This is only the beginning. Your family has betrayed you. You can't trust them even if they compliment you" (12:5-6).

In the second part of God's answer, Jeremiah is privileged by God to see that what has happened to him is a tragedy in miniature of what has happened to God.[xii] Yahweh has been abandoned by his people. "My inheritance," says the Lord, "has become to me like a lion in the forest. She roars at me; therefore I hate her" (12:8). In prayer the prophet and his God discover a common bond. As he prayed out his feelings of frustration and listened to God faithfully, he identified with the will of God.

This was not the only time Jeremiah prayed out his hate. A conspiracy sponsored by the religious leaders to discredit and ignore Jeremiah triggered a passionate, vehement prayer for vindication and vengeance (18:18-23). The spirit of the conspirators comes through in their rationale, "Come, let's make plans against Jeremiah; for the teaching of the law by the priest will not be lost, nor will counsel from the wise, nor the word from the prophets. So come, let's attack him with our tongues and pay no attention to anything he says" (18:18). Those in leadership decided that they had nothing to lose and everything to gain by silencing Jeremiah. Their thinking was especially perverse, because they claimed that the Word of the Lord would not suffer with Jeremiah out of the way. They conspired to "black ball" the Lord's prophet so they wouldn't have to put up with his teaching. Jeremiah blasted Judah's depraved leadership with a caustic invective to God that spared no one:

> But enough! Let their children starve!
> Let them be massacred in battle!
> Let their wives be childless and widowed,
> their friends die and their proud young men killed.
> Let cries of panic sound from their homes
> as you surprise them with war parties!
> They're all set to lynch me.
> The noose is practically around my neck!
> But you know all this, God.
> You know they're determined to kill me.
> Don't whitewash their crimes,
> don't overlook a single sin!
> Round the bunch of them up before you.
> Strike while the iron of your anger is hot!"
> (18:21-22; The Message)

It may be shocking for today's followers of Jesus Christ to realize that Jeremiah's prayer is far more biblical than our pious sounding cut-flower prayers. Jeremiah had more in common with Jesus, who declared, "I have come to cast fire on the earth" (Luke 12:49), than with popular, feel-good preachers who say, "Peace, peace, when there is no peace" (6:14; 8:11). At least Jeremiah is praying out his hate and expressing his moral outrage against those who hate God and deny his Word. At least he knew that he had enemies, whereas so many professing Christians, who identify more with the world than Christ, naively think that everybody loves them because they are such nice people. Jesus said, "Love your enemies and pray for them that persecute you" (Matt.5:44). "But loving enemies presupposes that we know that they are there, whether many or few, and have begun to identify them....Our hate is used by God to bring the enemies of life and salvation to notice, and then involve us in active compassion for the victims."[xiii]

Jeremiah's spiritual pain and moral outrage causes us to evaluate our identification with the Lord's will and purpose. Is our suffering due to our disobedience and faithlessness or is it due to our obedience and faithfulness? Do we experience in Christ the tragedy in miniature that God has endured because of sin? Jeremiah felt like "a gentle lamb led to the slaughter" so he prayed out his hate, but it was Jesus who fulfilled Isaiah's prophesy and showed us how to love.

> "He was oppressed and afflicted, yet he did not
> open his mouth; he was led like a lamb to the
> slaughter, and as a sheep before her shearers is
> silent, so he did not open his mouth" (Isa.53:7).

Praying our Loneliness (15:15-18)

The trigger for Jeremiah's first lament was an outright threat to his life, but there were other circumstances that caused him to lament his pain and feel his loss. The responsibility of delivering God's devastating message of judgment must have taken its toll on Jeremiah's life. Like a doctor bearing a grim diagnosis to an unsuspecting patient, Jeremiah was tasked with confronting his people with a message they didn't want to hear. No wonder he felt alienated and alone. He was sent on a mission impossible. He was told by the Lord not to pray for "this people," and that even if Moses and Samuel were to stand before the Lord, his "heart would not go out to this people" (7:16; 11:14; 14:11; 15:1).

Through prayer Jeremiah worked through his sorrow of alienation and tried to come to terms with his loneliness. Like Job, the reason for his suffering did not lie in any particular offense that he had done, but in faithfully doing what the Lord had called him to do. As if to suggest that money is the root of all evil, Jeremiah gave a one line defense of his innocence, "I have neither lent nor borrowed, yet everyone curses me" (15:10). He turned to the Lord as his only solace, praying, "You understand, O Lord; remember me and care for me." This was a remarkable starting point and one that Jeremiah *knew* to be true in his mind, but as the conclusion of his prayer shows he didn't *feel* it in his heart. As he prayed, he contemplated the reasons for his loneliness: "...I suffer reproach for your sake. When your words came, I ate them; they were my joy and my heart's delight, for I bear your name, O Lord God Almighty" (15:15-16). He *knew* he was alone for all the right reasons: "I never sat in the company of revelers, never made merry with them; I sat alone because your hand was on me and you had filled me with indignation" (15:17). But in his isolation he *felt* awful: "Why is my pain unending and my wound grievous and incurable?" In a clash between head and heart, between what he knew to be right and what he felt to be wrong, Jeremiah ended his prayer angrily, "Will you be to me like a deceptive brook, like a spring that fails?" (15:18).

We don't have to wait long to learn whether Jeremiah's disappointment with God was justified. It was one thing to lament his loneliness, but it was quite another to accuse God of letting him down. The Lord's response to Jeremiah was at first bracing, then affirming, "'If you repent, I will restore you that you may serve me; if you utter worthy, not worthless, words you will be my spokesman. Let this people turn to you, but you must not turn to them. I will make you a wall to this people, a fortified wall of bronze; they will fight against you but will not overcome you, for I am with you to rescue and save you,' declares the Lord. 'I will save you from the hands of the wicked and redeem you from the grasp of the cruel'" (15:19-21).

No matter how isolated and alienated Jeremiah felt, he had no excuse for sinking into self-pity and blaming God. The Lord said in effect, "Stop your whining. Don't dwell on your feelings, focus on my message. You don't want the company of these people anyway, in fact you need my protection from them. I will rescue, save, and redeem you from the wicked and ruthless." Eugene Peterson writes, "No one becomes human the way Jeremiah was human by posing in a posture of victory. It was his prayers, hidden but persistent, that brought him to the human wholeness and spiritual sensitivity that we want. What we do in secret determines the soundness of who we are in public. Prayer is the secret work that develops a life that is thoroughly authentic and deeply human" (Run with the Horses, 108). If the Lord is saying to Jeremiah in so many words, "Get over it," what is he saying to us? Are we ready to take in this word that squelches our tendency to blame God and strengthens our trust in his deliverance?

Praying our Despair (20:7-18)

Jeremiah's longest complaint was triggered by Pashhur, the senior priest in the Jerusalem temple and the official responsible for maintaining the temple's decorum and order. He heard Jeremiah's message when the prophet "stood in the court of the Lord's temple and said to all the people, 'This is what the Lord Almighty, the God of Israel, says: 'Listen! I am going to bring on this city and villages around it every disaster I pronounced against them, because they are stiff-necked and would not listen to my words'" (19:14-15). Jeremiah courageously preached the destruction of everything that the prominent and ever popular senior priest vowed to maintain. So it is no wonder that he reacted against Jeremiah and treated him like a common criminal, who needed to be taught a lesson that he wouldn't soon forget. Pashhur had Jeremiah beaten and put in the stocks for twenty-four hours at the Upper Gate of Benjamin at the Lord's temple, in order to humiliate the prophet and discredit his message. A badly beaten Jeremiah was put on display in a device designed to twist and contort the body. Added to his physical pain was the psychological pain of public ridicule, social embarrassment and personal mockery. Some of the bystanders may have mocked him with his own words by using a phrase that Jeremiah repeated in his message of judgment from time to time (6:25; 46:5; 49:29). "I hear many whispering, 'Terror on every side!' Report him! Let's report him!" (20:10). It appears that the people pulled a line from Jeremiah's message ("Terror on every side!") and used it as a catch phrase to taunt him.

However, if Pashhur thought that subjecting Jeremiah to public humiliation would silence the prophet or suppress his stern message he was wrong. On the very next day, when Jeremiah was released from the stocks, he fought back with a stinging indictment against Pashhur that must have had everyone talking before the day was out. "The Lord's name for you is not Pashhur," said Jeremiah, "but Magor-Missabib," which means "terror on every side." And he didn't stop with Pashhur's new name, he went on to announce to the senior priest that he would see many of his friends executed in the invasion and that he himself would go into exile to Babylon (20:4-6). By all accounts, Jeremiah had the last word, but the incident took a heavy psychological toll and triggered in him a deep-seated emotional reaction that drove him not only to prayer, but to despair. What follows is not for the spiritually faint-hearted nor for those who like their religion safely limited to pious platitudes.

Jeremiah's lament was intense, even vehement, right from the start. He began, "O Lord, you deceived me, and I was deceived; you overpowered me and prevailed" (20:7). The word for "deceived" is translated in Exodus 22:16 as "seduced" and in Judges 16:5 as "lured."xiv Using language which was both crude and offensive, Jeremiah complained bitterly that God had seduced him and forced himself upon him. Clearly, Jeremiah was at the breaking point. He had hit bottom. He was angry with God, angry with himself, and intent on cursing the day of his birth. It seems strikingly incongruous that Jeremiah should face Pashhur with such undaunted courage only to lash out against Yahweh in terms that border on contempt, if not blasphemy. It seems that way until we realize that hitting bottom emotionally does not rule out rising to the heights spiritually.

Jeremiah's encounter with Pashhur was extremely demanding physically and emotionally. It cost him dearly and it tested his character to the limit. To his credit,

Jeremiah did not break before the enemy. If he had done so, he would have failed in his mission. Instead he broke down before his "Commanding Officer," which by the grace of God he had the freedom to do. Authentic spirituality knows the difference between betrayal and lament, deception and depression, treachery and trust. Before God, no one can fake it to make it and Jeremiah didn't even try. He was bold before the enemy, but before Yahweh he was in despair. We can learn a lot from Jeremiah's example. If we were as bold before the world as Jeremiah was before Pashhur, our prayers might be as passionate as his.

The paradoxical nature of Jeremiah's prayer of despair continues with his understanding of his call. He attributed the reason for his persecution to "proclaiming violence and destruction." The fact of the matter, Jeremiah concluded, was obvious, "the Word of the Lord has brought me insult and reproach all day long" (20:8). Yet he refused to give up the one thing that caused his suffering. "But if I say," Jeremiah anguished, 'I will not mention him or speak any more in his name,' his word is in my heart like a burning fire, shut up in my bones. I am weary of holding it in; indeed, I cannot.'" (20:9). Instead of weakening his resolve to deliver the Word of the Lord, his prayer of despair literally forced him to understand its compelling inner drive, the fire in his bones, that could not be extinguished. Ironically, the expression of his despair demonstrated the intensity of his devotion to the Word of the Lord.

We are inclined to think that the most important part of any communication comes at the end, but to the Hebrew mind, the heart of the matter lies at the center. Jeremiah's prayer was no exception. In the middle of his lament, Jeremiah prayed out his relational anguish. "All my friends are waiting for me to slip, saying, 'Perhaps he will be deceived; then we will prevail over him and take our revenge on him.'" This is the painful problem that has wounded Jeremiah from the beginning. He felt alienated, alone, and estranged from everyone around him. Of course, it wasn't just that he was friendless. To be left alone, ignored and ostracized would have been hard enough, but Jeremiah was hated, betrayed, and plotted against, and all for the sake of Yahweh. Once again, the paradoxical nature of his prayer of despair comes through, because Jeremiah answered his relational anguish with a bold declaration of confidence in the Lord God.

> But the Lord is with me like a mighty warrior;
>> so my persecutors will stumble and not prevail.
> They will fail and be thoroughly disgraced;
>> their dishonor will never be forgotten.
> O Lord Almighty, you who examine the righteous
>> and probe the heart and mind,
>> let me see your vengeance upon them,
>> for to you I have committed my cause.

In the midst of his desperate relational pain he renewed his commitment to the Lord and then broke into song!

> Sing to the Lord! Give praise to the Lord!
> He rescues the life of the needy
> from the hands of the wicked. (20:11-13)

Singing praise to God doesn't seem to fit with a prayer of despair, nevertheless there it is at the center of Jeremiah's prayer. Perhaps it is easily overlooked by his shocking conclusion, but if we want to know Jeremiah's heart and the bedrock realities that he depended on we have to understand

Jeremiah's enduring commitment to the Lord who was with him "like a mighty warrior."

The final paradoxical aspect of Jeremiah's prayer is that his curse-filled conclusion does not indicate a weakened faith and trust in the Lord but a powerful empathy with the Lord's curse against life itself because of human sin and evil. Jeremiah concluded not by calling down curses on the wicked, but by calling down curses on himself. The flood gates of grief and despair poured out and he cursed the day of his birth, "Why did I ever come out of the womb to see trouble and sorrow and to end my days in shame?" (20:18). Like Job, Jeremiah questioned "Why?" He lashed out at the human condition. This was no sniveling, self-pitying whine, but a full throttle outburst. No bleeding heart "why me?" There is strength in every syllable, power in every line. The force of his lament is overwhelming. Jeremiah's lament is from the depths of his soul. It is like a hammer shattering excuses, explanations, and overtures of pity. We are reminded of God's words following the Fall. God cursed. God cursed his very own creation.

> "Cursed are you above all the livestock and all the wild animals! You will crawl on your belly and you will eat dust all the days of your life. And I will put enmity between you and the woman, and between your offspring and hers; he will crush your head, and you will strike his heel....Cursed is the ground because of you; through painful toil you will eat of it all the days of your life" (Gen.3:14-15,17).

"The curse is the affirmation of the fallen world by the Creator."[xv] Sin gives rise to enmity and evil, physical pain and spiritual suffering. We live between the curse and the promise. The curse is the reminder that God defines the good. The curse in the Garden shouts "No" to evil. God puts his foot down and shouts across the creation, across the cosmos, across all time. Sin is sin. Evil is evil. Cancer is not health, it's hell. God's curse defines and separates out the good from the evil, life from death. With his curse, God took sides against evil and so did Jeremiah. He cursed the life that God gave him to live, but he did not curse God. He cursed the miserable human condition and shared God's moral outrage against a fallen, broken, sin-twisted, evil world. In prayer Jeremiah echoed God's curse in the Garden of Eden.

If we were ever tempted to determine the Lord's calling for our lives according to our personality or temperament, Jeremiah's example would show us the error of our ways. If he had based God's call on his temperament or emotional equilibrium he never would have been obedient. Jeremiah did not *feel* like the ministry he was given, and at times he tried hard to resist it, but in the end, obedience won out in spite of inner doubts and external threats.

5. Bad News on Leadership

*"Woe to the shepherds who are
destroying and scattering the sheep of
my pasture!' declares the Lord. "*
Jeremiah 23:1

Bad leadership and Jeremiah's perseverance dominate this next section (chapters 21-28). If we plot this section it becomes obvious that chronological order was not the author's concern. Jeremiah focused on the subject of his message rather than a chronology of events. Although the book of Jeremiah was never intended to be a history lesson, it may be helpful to plot the history of this section to help us focus on the message. Tracking the time-line is difficult, but Jeremiah's critique comes through loud and clear.

Jeremiah's prime example of bad leadership begins with Zedekiah, Judah's last king before the exile (597-587 BC), and works backwards, but not in any strict chronological order. At the time, Jerusalem was under siege by the Babylonians, exactly as Jeremiah had prophesied (21:1-22:10). Jeremiah used Zedekiah to illustrate the kind of bad leadership that he was called of God to denounce.

Jeremiah's emphasis lies more on where he gave this message, at the palace of the king of Judah, than when he gave the message (22:1-10).

Next, with a brief comment, Jeremiah dismissed King Shallum, (another name for Jehoahaz), who reigned in Judah for only three months before he was exiled to Egypt where he died in 609 BC (22:11-12; see 2 Kings 23:33f.; 2 Chron.36:4). He then turned to Jehoiakim, elder brother of Shallum, appointed king by Egyptian Pharaoh Neco, who lived from 609 to 597 BC (22:13-23; see 2 Kings 23:34-24:6). Jeremiah's great temple sermon came at the beginning of Jehoiakim's reign (7:1-26; 26:1-6). His son, Jehoiachin became king in December 598 BC and after a mere three months was deported to Babylon as a royal hostage. Jeremiah dismissed Jehoiachin as "a despised, broken pot, an object no one wants" (22:24-30; see 2 Kings 25:27-30; Jer. 52:31-34). This description of Judah's kings sets the stage for the good news, when in contrast to these evil kings, God will raise up a successor to King David who is a true shepherd and he will be called, The Lord Our Righteousness (23:1-8).

Next in view, are the prophets (23:9-40). They are scrutinized by Jeremiah and found to be wicked, deceptive, wilful, and delusional. Then back again to the description of the kings for round two and Jeremiah's object lesson of the two baskets of figs (24:1-10). This took place after 597 BC when Jehoiachin was carried into Babylon and Zedekiah became king in Judah. Once again the editor works backwards. Jeremiah's summary pronouncement of judgment against Israel's shepherds occurred in 605 BC, during Jehoiakim's reign (25:1-38). Jeremiah had been hard at work for 23 years, which fits with the timing of his call in 627-628 BC.

Jeremiah's temple sermon (26:1-24; see 7:1-8:3) is referred to again and dated 690 BC during the reign of

Jehoiakim. This time the outraged reaction of the leadership against Jeremiah is emphasized. In 597 BC, Jeremiah dramatized Judah's need to submit to Babylonian rule under Nebuchadnezzar, by putting a yoke around his neck (27:1-22). His message contradicted the self-appointed prophets and popular priests who insisted on a message of false hope. This section concludes with Jeremiah once again turning his attention to the false prophets and to the prophet Hananiah in particular (28:1-17). The common theme running through this section focuses on bad leadership. Prophets, priests and kings conspired to wilfully and systematically oppose the Word of the Lord.

Getting Political

The timing of Zedekiah's request to Jeremiah underscores the illustrative nature of this section. Nebuchadnezzar, king of Babylon, had laid siege to Jerusalem. Conquest and exile were imminent (587 BC). Jeremiah began this section with Judah's long-awaited political climax, the final occupation and deportation that the prophet had been predicting for many years. He did this to demonstrate the moral and spiritual character of the house of David. King Zedekiah was fully aware of Jehoiachin's exile to Babylon ten years before (597 BC; 22:24-30). He had heard Jeremiah's "Good Figs, Bad Figs" message after the first exile, which stated categorically that God's blessing was for those who went into exile. The Word of the Lord through Jeremiah could not have been clearer. It was as simple as rotten fruit and sweet tasting fruit. The truth was as stark as black and white, red and green—right and wrong.

> "Like these good figs, I regard as good the
> exiles from Judah, whom I sent away from this

place to the land of the Babylonians. My eyes will watch over them for their good, and I will bring them back to the land. I will build them up and not tear them down; I will plant them and not uproot them. I will give them a heart to know me, that I am the Lord. They will be my people, and I will be their God, for they will return to me with all their heart."

"'But like the poor figs, which are so bad they cannot be eaten,' says the Lord, 'so I will deal with Zedekiah king of Judah, his officials and survivors from Jerusalem, whether they remain in this land or live in Egypt. I will make them abhorrent and an offense to all the kingdoms of the earth, a reproach and byword, an object of ridicule and cursing, wherever I banish them. I will send the sword, famine and plague against them until they are destroyed from the land I gave to them and their fathers.'" (24:5-10).

Zedekiah knew that Jeremiah had been delivering this same message since the days of Josiah. Everyone knew that in the first year of Nebuchadnezzar's reign in Babylon, when Jehoiakim, Josiah's son, ruled in Judah, Jeremiah had prophesied that there would be seventy years of captivity (25:1-38). This captivity was calculated to extend from the fourth year of Jehoiakim's reign, 605 BC, to the time of Ezra and Nehemiah and the return of the exiles ca. 536 BC (Zech 1:12; 2 Chr 36:20-23). Everyone knew that Jeremiah was nearly killed for delivering his momentous "temple sermon" during the early days of Jehoiakim's reign when he laid down the Lord's ultimatum (26:1-24; 7:1-8:3).

How could Zedekiah forget the public spectacle of Jeremiah walking around Jerusalem shouldering a heavy yoke? How could he forget the embarrassment of Jeremiah sending word to the kings of Edom, Moab, Ammon, Tyre and Sidon, through their ambassadors, that the Lord of Israel was handing over all their countries, together with Judah, "to my servant Nebuchadnezzar king of Babylon" (27:6)? According to the prophet himself, he could not have delivered the Word of the Lord more boldly and graphically: "I gave the same message to Zedekiah king of Judah. I said, 'Bow your neck under the yoke of the king of Babylon; serve him and his people, and you will live. Why will you and your people die by the sword, famine and plague with which the Lord has threatened any nation that will not serve the king of Babylon? Do not listen to the words of the prophets who say to you, 'You will never serve the king of Babylon,' for they are prophesying lies to you'" (27:12-14).

One of those lying prophets was Hananiah, who publicly confronted Jeremiah in the temple and declared that the Lord had told him that in two years the yoke of Babylonian rule would be broken (594 BC; 28:1-4). Zedekiah must have heard the irony and sarcasm in Jeremiah's response to Hananiah when Jeremiah said,

> "Wonderful! Would that it were true—that God would validate your preaching by bringing the Temple furnishings and all the exiles back from Babylon. But listen to me, listen closely. Listen to what I tell both of you and all the people here today: The old prophets, the ones before our time, preached judgment against many countries and kingdoms, warning of war and disaster and plague. So any prophet who preaches that everything is just fine and there's nothing to worry about stands out like sore

thumb. We'll wait and see. If it happens, it happens—and then we'll know that God sent him" (28:6-9; The Message).

Hananiah should have quit, but he preceded to remove Jeremiah's yoke and break it up in pieces as he repeated his prophesy that Babylon would be gone in two years. Jeremiah turned on his heels and left the scene, but a few days later he confronted Hananiah with the Word of the Lord. Jeremiah's message to Judah and the surrounding nations was unambiguous, "This is what the Lord says: You have broken a wooden yoke, but in its place you will get a yoke of iron" (28:13). He was just as direct to Hananiah, "Listen, Hananiah! The Lord has not sent you, yet you have persuaded this nation to trust in lies. Therefore, this is what the Lord says: 'I am about to remove you from the face of the earth. This very year you are going to die, because you have preached rebellion against the Lord'" (28:15-16). Hananiah thought he was preaching a message of peace, but in fact, he was preaching rebellion from the Lord. Two months later he was dead (28:17).

King Zedekiah was without excuse. He knew where Jeremiah stood and he knew what the will of the Lord was. Zedekiah was well aware of the great temple sermon, and Jeremiah's prophesy of the seventy year captivity was public knowledge. The vivid object lessons of figs and the yoke around Jeremiah's neck made the Word of the Lord clear. Nevertheless, Zedekiah had the audacity to send a delegation to Jeremiah, saying, "Inquire now of the Lord for us because Nebuchadnezzar king of Babylon is attacking us. Perhaps the Lord will perform wonders for us as in times past so that he will withdraw from us" (21:2). Once again, Jeremiah was forced to repeat what the Lord had told him to say for so many years, "I myself will fight against you with an outstretched hand and a mighty arm in anger and fury and great wrath" (21:5).

Jeremiah likened his message to a consuming fire and "a hammer that breaks a rock to pieces" (23:29), and by now the reader may be forgiven for thinking that the fire had consumed everything and the rock must have been smashed into powder. The unrelenting nature of Jeremiah's message may cause some to say, "Enough, already. You have made your point!" But the issue was not that Jeremiah needed to *get over it*, it was that the people needed to *get it*. What they didn't get was that God was not some tribal deity that guaranteed their protection. What they didn't understand was that their verbal religiosity did not impress Yahweh who sought justice on behalf of the poor and oppressed. They failed to grasp that their selfish and materialistic aspirations contradicted God's plan for a just and righteous society.

Does the repetitive nature of Jeremiah's message pound away at our propensity to marry religious and political sentiments. In spite of everything Jeremiah stood for, Zedekiah persisted in asking Jeremiah for God's blessing and hoping for an eleventh hour miraculous rescue. Zedekiah seemed oblivious to his own spiritual rebellion and his insistence upon using God for his own political purposes. By blending God-and-country and mixing his religious sentiments with his nationalistic aspirations, Zedekiah proudly espoused a civil religion. But it was a religion that refused to pay attention to the Word of the Lord (37:2). Even though he consistently chose religious pluralism, hedonism, and materialism, Zedekiah believed that God was on his side and success was assured. Undoubtedly Zedekiah had plenty of religious support for his point-of-view. The delegation he sent to Jeremiah included Pashhur son of Malkijah and a royal official, (not to be confused with the Pashhur (20:1) with whom Jeremiah clashed twenty years earlier) and Zephaniah son of Maaseiah, a priest, who was asked by Zedekiah on several occasions to seek Jeremiah's support (37:3). Zedekiah made the mistake common among egotistical leaders of transferring his own motives and modus operandi to Jeremiah and reasoning that Jeremiah could be wooed with pseudo respect and placated with artificial deference. But the prophet was neither impressed nor intimidated. They wanted Jeremiah's support and blessing, but they didn't want to listen to his preaching.

As we have said before, the leadership in Jerusalem staunchly supported the temple and used religion as a rallying cry. They were quick to say, "the temple of the Lord, the temple of the Lord, the temple of the Lord" (7:4). They repeated the phrase, "As surely as the Lord lives," and they pretended to turn to the Lord. But there was nothing righteous about their actions nor genuine about their motives (2:27; 5:2). They were all talk, leading Jeremiah to complain to God, "You are always on their lips but far from their hearts" (12:2).

Following his pronouncement of judgment, Jeremiah confronted Judah's royal line with a life or death choice (21:8-9), a clarion call for justice (21:11-14; 22:1-5), and a rebuke of their materialism (22:13-17). Jeremiah was led by the Lord to deliver an either/or message that was reminiscent of the challenge Moses gave to the Israelites (Deut.30:15,19): "This is what the Lord says: 'See, I am setting before you the way of life and the way of death" (21:8). But the leadership felt no compulsion to choose. They wanted it both ways. They wanted to copy the ways of the world, condone pagan practices, conform to the spirit of the times but also maintain affiliation with their religious heritage. Jeremiah challenged their both/and thinking with simple dualisms, stark alternatives, red and green logic, black and white choices. Obedience was a cut and dry decision. Faithfulness was an up or down vote. There was no in-between gray areas that allowed Judah's leaders to please Yahweh and also appease Baal, or exploit the poor and rescue the poor. They had to choose one or the other. They had simple options, either eat rotten figs or eat sweetly ripened figs. The choice was theirs.

Like the "shepherds" in Jeremiah's day there are religious leaders today who mock what they call the "simplistic bifurcation" that pits "us" against "them" in matters related to biblical faith and practice. I imagine that they would condemn Jeremiah for his "destructive binary oppositions" and his "troublesome polarization." They speak of "inclusivity" and "wholeness" and assure us that radically divergent theological perspectives belong together. They intentionally confuse racial and ethnic diversity with radical pluralism. Their watchword is "shalom" but they define peace "merely as the absence of turmoil and social conflict, and not as the triumph of divine righteousness among people."[xvi] They decry the macro-dichotomy that threatens to split every major historic American denomination in two, but they refuse to draw a line between belief and unbelief, fidelity and idolatry, sexual purity and sexual immorality. They fail to distinguish between conforming to the spirit of the times and submitting to the Word of the Lord.

There is a place for both/and thinking *within* a biblically rooted, Christ-centered world-view. Certain biblical truths ought to be held in tension. For example we believe in the total depravity of humankind *and* the evidence of God's image even in the vilest sinner. We accept God's unconditional, sovereign control and election *and* affirm the freedom and responsibility of the person to respond to God. We believe in the salvation God provides through Christ's atoning sacrifice on the cross for all those who are elected *and* in the universal invitation of the gospel--that whosoever will may come. We believe in the irresistible grace of God *and* the human freedom of choice to reject as well as accept the gospel. We believe in the perseverance of the saints *and* we strive to remain faithful to the end. This biblical wholeness, which works to hold in tension truths affirmed in the Bible, rests on an exclusive commitment to Christ and his word.

No one emphasized the either/or alternative more than Jesus. We might prefer an indecisive "maybe," or a kind of middle-of-the-road, *whatever* belief system, but Jesus did not give us that option. What we get in Jesus' Sermon on the Mount is a series of either/or alternatives: two ways (broad and narrow), two teachers (false and true), two pleas (words and deeds) and finally two foundations (sand and rock). Jesus ends his message with a parable about two kinds of builders: one who builds on the rock and one who builds on the sand. Jesus established a clear line and a sharp contrast between wisdom and foolishness. Jeremiah was compelled by the Lord to do the same thing.

Whether or not Jeremiah's call for justice fell on deaf ears, the prophet persisted in confronting Judah's kings with God's top priority for leadership. All talk and no action compelled Jeremiah to say to "the royal house of Judah, 'Hear the Word of the Lord; O house of David, this is what the Lord says: 'Administer justice every morning; rescue from the hand of the oppressor the one who has been robbed, or my wrath will break out and burn like fire because of the evil you have done—burn with no one to quench it" (21:11-12).

Jeremiah was known not only for his temple sermon, but for his palace manifesto. The Lord said, "Go down to the palace of the king of Judah and proclaim this message there: 'Hear the Word of the Lord, O king of Judah, you who sit on David's throne—you, your officials and your people who come through these gates." The Word of the Lord was as necessary to politics as it was to spirituality. It belonged not only in the temple, but in society at large. Any compartmentalization of life that ruled out the Word of the Lord would have been foreign to Jeremiah.

It is important to note that the recipients of this message range from the king to the officials to the people. Jeremiah gave this manifesto in a hierarchical society ruled by a king, yet he stressed its implications for all people. If this was true then, how much more is it true today? Democratization has made us think and act like kings. Society has substituted one myth for another, the myth of the divine right of kings for the myth of self rule. The rise of the imperial self is just as much a danger to biblical justice as any autocratic king. The sovereign self, with its blatant self-seeking individualism is no better for seeking justice than the law of the jungle and the survival of the fittest. To be ruled by the competitive market place is definitely not the same as being ruled by the will of the Lord.

The straightforward character of Jeremiah's plea for justice has a long tradition in God's Salvation History story. And as the prophets before him stressed, the just and right thing to do is plain to those who seek to obey God's will. Jeremiah spoke plainly, "This is what the Lord says: Do what is just and right. Rescue from the hand of his oppressor the one who has been robbed. Do no wrong or violence to the alien, the fatherless or the widow, and do not shed innocent blood in this place" (22:3). Yet human nature's sinful tendency to confuse God's simple justice was as readily apparent then as it is today. The "powers that be" from the ancient king to the modern existential self make justice out to be a mystery.

Jeremiah exposed one of the obvious sins that made justice more difficult when he confronted King Jehoiakim's materialism:

> "Woe to him who builds his palace by unrighteousness, his upper rooms by injustice, making his countrymen work for nothing, not paying them for their labor. He says, 'I will build myself a great palace with spacious upper rooms.' So he makes large windows in it, panels it with cedar and decorates it in red. Does it make you a king to have more and more cedar? Did not your father have food and drink? He did what was right and just, so all went well with him" (22:13-15).

Jeremiah contended with Jehoiakim that if he wanted to do justice, he only had to look to the example of his father, Josiah, who had "defended the cause of the poor and needy." "But your eyes and your heart," accused Jeremiah, "are set only on dishonest gain, on shedding innocent blood and on oppression and extortion" (22:16-17). The prophets insisted that doing what was just and right was not nearly as complicated and idealistic as people blinded by greed and selfish interests make it out to be.

One final theme that runs through Jeremiah's discussion of royal leadership is the question of legacy and how Judah's kings should be respected and remembered. Jeremiah was sensitive to the dignity and honor due to a king who fulfilled his leadership responsibilities. In his palace manifesto, he promised, "For if you are careful to carry out these commands, then kings who sit on David's throne will come through the gates of this palace, riding in chariots and on horses, accompanied by their officials and their people" (22:4). This was not an appeal to the royal ego, but a picture of the respect afforded those who sought to serve the people according to God's will rather than their own selfish interests and the interests of a ruling elite. Sadly, Judah's kings chose a different legacy and Jeremiah vividly described their fate: Zedekiah's execution (21:7), Jehoahaz's (Shallum) captivity and death (22:11-12), Jehoiakim's burial fit for a donkey (22:19), and Jehoiachin's good riddance-exile (22:24-30).

Confronting the Religious Establishment

Judah's kings were bad, but her prophets and priests were worse and the nation's demise was attributed more to the failure of its spiritual leaders than the corruption of its political leaders. It is bad enough to wield power for selfish gain, but to purport to speak for God when the message is only human opinion and a wish dream is far worse. It is one thing to be useless, it is another thing to be deceptive. It is better to ignorantly say, "I don't know," than it is to arrogantly lead people astray. Judah's kings exploited the people, but Judah's prophets and priests deceived the people, because they exchanged the truth for a lie. They were the ones responsible for spreading "ungodliness" throughout the land (23:15). But if they had "stood in my council," said the Lord, "and proclaimed my words to my people," then "they would have turned them from their evil ways and from their evil deeds" (23:22).

Jeremiah was overwhelmed by God's verdict against the religious leaders. "My head is reeling," he complained, "my limbs are limp, I'm staggering like a drunk, seeing double from too much wine—And all because of his holy words" (23:9; The Message). "The land is full of adulterers," cried Jeremiah. "'Both prophet and priest are godless; even in my temple I find their wickedness,' declares the Lord" (23:11). Jeremiah charged that the prophets of Jerusalem were even worse than the prophets of Samaria (Israel) who practiced Baal worship, because "they commit adultery and live a lie" (23:14). The implication is that they committed the full range of illicit sexual relations from lust and marital infidelity to homosexual practice (see Gen.19:4-5). "They are all like Sodom to me; the people of Jerusalem are like Gomorrah," declared the Lord (23:14). For these leaders, spiritual idolatry and sexual infidelity went hand-in-hand. Their teaching and their life-style were as dangerous to the people as if they had poisoned Jerusalem's drinking water and polluted the land.

The religious rhetoric of these false prophets and bad priests remind us of some modern church leaders who advocate so-called sexual freedom and hold out false hope for success and self-fulfillment. "They speak visions from their own minds, not from the mouth of the Lord," declared the Lord. "They keep saying to those who despise me, 'The Lord says: you will have peace.' And to all who follow the stubbornness of their hearts they say, 'No harm will come to you'" (23:16-17). This is an apt description of the modern church leader who commends various forms of sexual fulfillment outside of a marriage commitment between a man and a woman. The order of the day appears to have been "feel-good" sermons based on popular sentiment coupled with an affirming attitude regardless of what the Word of the Lord said. "They preach their 'Everything Will Turn Out Fine' sermon to congregations with no taste for God, their

'Nothing Bad Will Ever Happen to You' sermon to people who are set in their own ways" (23:17; The Message). Their refusal to stand in the council of the Lord is not only blatant but stupid. They act as if the Lord is oblivious to their disobedience and unaware of their indifference to his word. "'Am I only a God nearby,' declares the Lord, 'and not a God far away? Can anyone hide in secret places so I cannot see him?' declares the Lord. 'Do not I fill heaven and earth?' declares the Lord" (23:23-24).

The false prophets of Jeremiah's day were visionaries who fed the people a steady diet of excitement and hype. They preached enthusiastically, "I had a dream! I had a dream!' and then proceeded to offer "the delusions of their own minds" (23:25-26). They preached their seven steps to success and their five ways to a happy sex life. They presented their four keys to healthy self-esteem and revealed their ten best kept secrets for church growth. All the while the Lord assessed their wish-dream sermons as a ploy to keep from remembering what really counted. "'They think the dreams they tell one another will make my people forget my name, just as their fathers forgot my name through Baal worship. Let the prophet who has a dream tell his dream, but let the one who has my word speak it faithfully. For what has straw to do with grain?' declares the Lord" (23:27-28). The comparison between straw and grain was an apt one. Straw makes fodder for animals, but it doesn't make bread for humans. These delusional sermons were at best useless distractions and at worst major deceptions. In any case they did not feed the soul. In contrast to their people-pleasing sermons, the Word of the Lord was like a consuming fire and a hammer that breaks a rock in pieces (23:29).

Another characteristic of these false prophets was that they plagiarized each other's work. The ever-escalating pressure to come up with something new and exciting meant that they copied the *next thing* from one another and then claimed it came from the Lord. "'Therefore,' declares the Lord, 'I am against the prophets who steal from one another words supposedly from me'" (23:30). Perhaps this sober line should be remembered as a warning to pastors who run to expensive conferences hoping to stay abreast of the latest trends and bring back a message of excitement for their congregations.

Jeremiah's final description of these false prophets details the Lord's disgust with their frequent attempts to discuss his word yet their flagrant refusal to discern his will. Asaph's lament fits Jeremiah's picture of the false prophets, "Their mouths lay claim to heaven, and their tongues take possession of the earth" (Ps.73:9). Or, as Jeremiah complained to God, "You are always on their lips but far from their hearts" (12:2). Like the false teachers described by the apostle Paul, they were "always learning but never able to acknowledge the truth" (2 Tim.3:7). Their constant references to the *will* of the Lord or the *burden* of the Lord or the *vision* of the Lord, only served to hide the fact that they were reduced to sharing human opinion and speculation.

Apparently they loved to debate the Scriptures, discuss religion, and talk about their spiritual feelings, but they refused to accept and obey the Word of the Lord. So Jeremiah was led to call for a moratorium on preaching the Word of the Lord, saying, "But you must not mention 'the oracle [burden] of the Lord' again, because everyone's own word becomes the oracle and so you distort the words of the living God, the Lord Almighty, our God" (23:36). Nevertheless, the false prophets persisted in claiming that their opinions were the Word of the Lord in spite of being warned not to. It was those who pretended to know the will of God who would find out soon enough that judgment was the will of God for them. God's verdict was final, "I will bring upon you everlasting disgrace—everlasting shame that will not be forgotten" (23:40).

Parable and Prophet

For two important reasons Jeremiah's attack against Judah's bad leadership causes the reader to think of Jesus Christ. Once again we see that the heart of the matter comes at the center of the section. In the middle of his description of evil kings and false prophets, Jeremiah issued a startling promise of hope, "'The days are coming,' declares the Lord, 'when I will raise up to David a righteous Branch, a King who will reign wisely and do what is just and right in the land. In his days Judah will be saved and Israel will live in safety. This is the name by which he will be called: The Lord Our Righteousness" (23:5-6). Like a good shepherd, this coming King "will gather the remnant of my flock out of all the countries where I have driven them and will bring them back to their pasture, where they will be fruitful and increase in number" (23:3). From Jeremiah's perspective Israel's redemption from Egypt was to be eclipsed one day by Israel's redemption from exile in Babylon (23:7-8). Both the exodus and the exile were key stages on the road to redemption through the Cross of Jesus Christ.

From the prophet who bore the burden of such bad news came unexpected good news that, in spite of bad leadership, the Lord still rules over his people and he will save them. There is hope for the future because of Yahweh's determination to raise up a descendent of David, who will be called "The Lord Our Righteousness." Unlike Zedekiah, who lived in opposition to the meaning of his name, "The

Lord is Righteousness," the King who is coming will fulfill the meaning of his name, because he will reign wisely and do what is just and right. The messianic nature of this prophecy is emphasized in several ways. Jeremiah's phrase "the days are coming" points forward to God's climactic revelation. The reference to "a righteous Branch" recalls Isaiah's messianic promise, "A shoot will come up from the stump of Jesse; from his roots a Branch will bear fruit" (Isa.11:1). And the name, The Lord Our Righteousness, does not point away from the individual to God as we would expect, but to the individual as God. This title may have been in the apostle Paul's mind when he referred to Christ Jesus, "who has become for us wisdom from God—that is, our righteousness, holiness and redemption," especially when his next thought quotes from Jeremiah, "Let him who boasts boast in the Lord" (1 Cor.1:30-31; Jer 9:24).

It is not only Jeremiah's messianic prophecy that makes us think of Jesus, but Jeremiah's life that forms a striking parallel to Jesus life. Just as Jesus debated the scribes and Pharisees and used the strongest language to rebuke them, so did Jeremiah before him. Jeremiah serves as a parable of Jesus, because he makes us think of Jesus. The debate among the officials of Judah over whether Jeremiah should die after delivering his temple sermon is strikingly reminiscent of the debate that raged some 600 years later among the scribes and Pharisees over whether or not Jesus should die. When we read that "the priests, the prophets and all the people seized him and said, 'You must die!' it is not difficult to think of Jesus when the crowd shouted, "Crucify him, crucify him!" (Jer 26:8; Mt 27:22-23). Just as Pilate testified to Jesus' innocence (John 19:4), some of the officials declared *"to the priests and the prophets"* that Jeremiah should not be sentenced to death, because "he has spoken to us in the name of the Lord our God" (26:16). Citing the prophet Micah during the reign of Hezekiah (716-687 BC) as a precedent, officials actually quoted what Micah had said about Jerusalem (Mic.1:1; 3:12). They determined that since Hezekiah didn't kill Micah, Jeremiah should not be sentenced to death.

How did the book of Jeremiah help shape Jesus' self-understanding? Did the ancient prophet's experience of evil kings and false prophets help prepare Jesus for his encounter with the political and religious leaders that sought to kill him? When Jeremiah faced his accusers with calm resolve and firm conviction, he spoke in a manner that makes us think of Jesus before Pilate. "As for me," Jeremiah said, "I am in your hands; do with me whatever you think is good and right. Be assured, however, that if you put me to death, you will bring the guilt of innocent blood on yourselves and on this city and on those who live in it, for in truth the Lord has sent me to you to speak all these words in your hearing" (26:14-15).

In God's great salvation history story, Jeremiah stands as parable and prophet. His life serves as a parable of Jesus, foreshadowing the life and work of the Messiah. His messianic prophecy leads us straight to the Gospel of John and the life of Christ. In a single descriptive line Jesus combined the prophecy and the parable. He identified himself as the descendent of David and the suffering servant, the coming King and the crucified Lord, when he said, "I am the good shepherd. The good shepherd lays down his life for the sheep" (John 10:11). In the midst of so much bad news about the leadership and spiritual condition of his people, Jeremiah delivered his message of hope in anticipation of the gospel of Jesus Christ.

6. Hope and a Future

*"For I know the plans I have for you,' declares the
Lord, 'plans to prosper you and not to harm you,
plans to give you hope and a future. Then you will call
upon me and come and pray to me, and I will listen to
you. You will seek me and find me when you seek me
with all your heart.'"* Jeremiah 29:11-13

In 597 BC, thousands of Israel's leaders, soldiers, artisans
and skilled craftsmen, were taken to Babylon in the first
wave of exiles (52:28; 2 Kings 24:8-17). This first group
included Jehoiachin, who succeeded Jehoiakim, and other
notables, such as Daniel and Ezekiel (Dan. 1:1-6; Ezek. 1:2).
They crossed the 550 miles of barren wasteland from
Jerusalem to Babylon on foot and under armed guard. We
would be naive if we thought this was not an ordeal of great
suffering and privation.

Jeremiah's famous words of hope and promise (29:11-
14) introduce the highpoint of his entire prophecy. This
section has been called the book of consolation (29:1-33:26)
because it describes the end of suffering, the joy of salvation,
and the promise of a New Covenant. Jeremiah promised
that the days of uprooting, upheaval and tearing down would

end, and a new day would begin, a time to build and plant. According to Jeremiah, Israel's future hope depended not on the people left behind in Judah, but upon those who had been carried into exile by Nebuchadnezzar. His prophecy countered the prevailing belief that Yahweh would never abandon Judah and in the end Jerusalem would be spared. King Zedekiah was convinced that God would perform wonders to save Judah (21:2) and the prophet Hananiah was not alone in prophesying that Babylon's conquest would be short-lived (28:2-3).

To the political and religious leadership Jeremiah's message sounded like cowardly capitulation, a case of outright treason. How could a true Israelite boldly declare to Zedekiah, "Bow your neck under the yoke of the king of Babylon; serve him and his people, and you will live" (27:12)? No king wants to be told to give up and surrender, but that was exactly what Jeremiah insisted he must do. For close to 30 years Jeremiah had been led by the Lord to prophesy the conquest of Jerusalem. Right from the start, he envisioned foreign kings setting up their thrones at the gates of Jerusalem (1:15). He announced victory for the besieging army (4:16; 6:22-26) and exile for Jerusalem's inhabitants, saying, "As you have forsaken me and served foreign gods in your own land, so now you will serve foreigners in a land not your own" (5:19). Jeremiah declared, "All Judah will be carried into exile, carried completely away" (13:19).

From a human perspective, in a competitive dog-eat-dog world, Jeremiah's message was a betrayal of Judah's ethnic pride, religious hope, and official leadership. He advocated surrender to the invading forces on grounds that Judah needed to go through judgment and endure exile before it could experience God's salvation. The Exodus, when Yahweh brought the Israelites up out of Egypt, was about to be superseded by the Exile (23:7-8). Both the Exodus and the Exile are turning points in Salvation History that serve as signposts on the way to the Cross. They are revelatory paradigms modeling and projecting God's redemptive strategy of expiation and propitiation. Israel in bondage is the prototype of a world in sin. Even as I am a microcosm of a world in sin.

We are lost in sin and we cannot save ourselves. We are rebels fighting against our liberation. Thus, Jeremiah's message was not as it appeared to Judah's leaders, a betrayal, but a hidden blessing that promised salvation. His message was all about judgment and redemption. Jeremiah explained that the exile was intended by God to move people to realize their need and turn to God for salvation. What was true then is still true today; in order for us to be raised up we have to be brought down. We have to come to terms with our captivity in order to experience freedom. The worst form of slavery is when slaves don't know they're enslaved. The exile helped the people see that they were bent on idolatry, addicted to adultery, and stuck in patterns of disobedience. They had to be taken out of their comfort zone in order to see how far they had wandered from faithfulness. Their only hope for deliverance rested in turning to God.

As we have seen, the dissonance between popular expectations and Jeremiah's prophetic ministry provoked serious opposition and endangered his life. The tensions Jeremiah encountered throughout his ministry remind us of the tensions Jesus encountered when he entered Jerusalem on Palm Sunday. Messianic fervor was running high and the crowd's loud cheers and hosannas reflected popular expectations. Jesus chose a powerful messianic symbol when he rode into Jerusalem on a colt. The people were looking for a political savior who would rally the nation and throw off the yoke of Roman oppression. They wanted someone who would fight for them, lead them out of bondage, and give them back their pride. In the excitement of a large crowd singing praises, waving palm branches, and laying down their cloaks in the dust, Jesus looked like a good candidate to lead a popular uprising against Rome. What no one in the crowd expected, including his disciples, was that Jesus had "arranged that his coronation take place on a cross."[xvii] In Jeremiah's day, salvation was on the other side of the exile; in Jesus' day it was on the other side of the Cross. In the mind of God, the two events are linked. Going through the exile proved to be a type or a pattern for living under the Cross, reminding us that "the gospel of Jesus Christ is more political than anyone imagines, but in a way that no one guesses."[xviii]

Good News for Captives

"God loves you and has a wonderful plan for your life," is certainly true, but how we interpret these words is critical. Many suffer delusional ideas when it comes to God's plan for their lives. Their mind seems bent on happiness and security issues. They immediately think of God's direction for their individual lives in terms of education, career, marriage and family. They *want* to interpret God's promise as a supernatural guarantee that offers them personal peace, physical security, economic success and inner significance. And when that kind of spiritualized success does not materialize they are disappointed with God. It is often unclear whether or not there is a distinction between a worldly strategy for self-fulfillment and Jesus' strategy for self-fulfillment. The "wonderful plan" seems to have little to do with taking up a cross and following Jesus and more to do with a false gospel of health and wealth. They forget that

Jesus said, "If anyone would come after me, he must deny himself and take up his cross and follow me. For whoever wants to save his life will lose it, but whoever loses his life for me will find it" (Matt.16:24-25).

Jeremiah sent an open letter to the first wave of exiles in 594 BC to challenge them to accept the hard work ahead and to warn them against delusional alternatives. His letter is another example of God's redemptive reversal which we have come to expect in salvation history. It is consistent with the principle that the first shall be last and the last shall be first. Instead of siding with those who stayed behind in Judah, God sided with the exiles. The future belonged to a remnant that God would call out of captivity. In the middle of what must have been a very difficult time for the exiles, Jeremiah delivered God's message of hope:

> "'For I know the plans I have for you,' declares the Lord, 'plans to prosper you and not to harm you, plans to give you hope and a future. Then you will call upon me and come and pray to me, and I will listen to you. You will seek me and find me when you seek me with all your heart. I will be found by you,' declares the Lord, 'and will bring you back from captivity. I will gather you from all the nations and places where I have banished you,' declares the Lord, 'and will bring you back to the place from which I carried you into exile'" (29:11-14).

Jeremiah's Spirit-inspired letter not only helped the exiles embrace God's plan, but it helps us who follow the Lord Jesus Christ to understand and obey God's plan for our lives. Jeremiah instructed the exiles in seven critical truths about the plan of God. All seven apply to the people of God today.

First, God's plan is revealed in his Word. Jeremiah's letter to the exiles and his postscript to Shemaiah is punctuated eighteen times with references to the Word of the Lord. Every thought is rooted in God's word and accredited with the sanction, thus *declares the Lord*. Jeremiah is a great example of what the apostle Paul affirmed when he said, "We demolish arguments and every pretension that sets itself up against the knowledge of God, and we take captive every thought to make it obedient to Christ" (2 Cor.10:4-5). To base the will of God on human speculation, opinions and feelings, is to fall victim to the spirit of the times and the mood of the moment. But to establish God's will on the solid ground of God's revelation is to live on a firm foundation that weathers the storms of life and the volatility of feelings. The Word of the Lord defines the long obedience in the same direction, apart from which we are constantly wandering down dead ends and dark alleys.

What Paul said of himself could be said of Jeremiah, "I did not come with eloquence or superior wisdom as I proclaimed to you the testimony about God" (1 Cor.2:1). Jeremiah did not come to negotiate but to announce. His primary responsibility was to proclaim rather than persuade, to deliver rather than debate. He repeatedly reiterated that the message he gave was not his own by way of invention or speculation but his by order of the Lord Almighty. What if we were as compelled to receive and obey the Word of the Lord, as Jeremiah was to give it? It was like fire in his bones (20:9).

Second, God's plan integrates the reality of pain and suffering into the gift of salvation. In the introduction to this section, we are told that Jeremiah's letter was sent to the leaders and the people whom "Nebuchadnezzar had carried into exile from

Jerusalem to Babylon," but in the letter itself, Jeremiah credits the Lord God with carrying the people into exile (29:1, 4). Who was responsible for the people's suffering in captivity, Nebuchadnezzar or the Lord Almighty? On the one hand, Nebuchadnezzar was responsible for this cruel and evil captivity, but on the other hand, Jeremiah saw the king of Babylon as God's instrument of judgment to punish Judah for their spiritual apostasy, disobedience and rebellion. It should also be said that Jeremiah was not afraid to declare publicly that Babylon would be judged harshly for their oppression of Israel (50:1f).

To credit the Lord God with responsibility for the captivity put a distinct but necessary twist to the meaning of suffering. And even as cruel and inhumane as the suffering was, it was the tragic consequence Jeremiah had prophesied because of Judah's constant rejection of the Word of the Lord and rebellion against God's ways. Judah had brought this captivity upon herself. No understanding of the will of God that failed to integrate this suffering could be called a wonderful plan. Jeremiah understood this suffering as necessary in God's redemptive plan to bring people back to a saving dependence upon the Lord God. Undoubtedly many of the exiles were disappointed with God. It is safe to assume that there was talk about being abandoned by God and deserted by him in their hour of greatest need. But they had no excuse. They had themselves to blame, rather than God to resent, for the captivity.

God takes credit for the consequences of evil actions, because judgment itself is a means of grace driving us back to God. There are two kinds of suffering, the suffering we experience as a direct result of our sin and the suffering we endure because we live in a sinful and evil world, but there is only one purpose for suffering and that is to move us to

God. All suffering has a redemptive purpose, to lead both sinner and victim, back to God in total dependence upon his grace and mercy. When we follow the sinful inclinations of our heart, God gives us up to the consequences of our motives and actions, so that we might experience the tragedy of that "freedom" and turn to God. As long as we refuse to acknowledge our *captivity* we will never be released from the bondage of sin and death. Until we understand that the wages of sin is death we will never to turn to God for the gift of eternal life through Christ Jesus our Lord (Rom.6:23).

Third, God's plan leads us to obey his will today in the normal course of ordinary life. Knowing the will of God is not a secret that needs to be discovered, but a command that needs to be obeyed. It is not about figuring out the future; it is about faithfulness in the present. Knowing the will of God is not so much about choosing a college, a career, or a spouse, but choosing the path of obedience and devotion that the living God has clearly laid out in his word. Life is not a maze of right turns and wrong turns, but a marathon of trust and dependence.

Jeremiah's letter to the exiles is a great illustration of this principle. He told them to live into the future by obeying God today. The will of God was simple and plain: "Build houses and settle down; plant gardens and eat what they produce. Marry and have sons and daughters; find wives for your sons and give your daughters in marriage, so that they too may have sons and daughters. Increase in number there; do not decrease" (29:5). In other words, ordinary life was meant to be the proving ground of faithfulness. They were meant to get to work, build relationships and leave the future in God's hands. Trust in Yahweh was to be worked out in community through work, marriage, and parenting.

This spiritual direction recalls the apostle Paul's exhortation to the church, when he wrote, "We hear that some among you are idle. They are not busy; they are busybodies. Such people we command and urge in the Lord Jesus Christ, to settle down and earn the bread they eat. And as for you, brothers and sisters, never tire of doing what is right" (2 Thess. 3:11-13). The exile afforded a new opportunity for the chosen people of God to discover all over again what it meant to live faithfully and obediently. The stranglehold of false spirituality, self-indulgent materialism and sexual promiscuity, that had squeezed the life out of Jerusalem, had been broken in Babylon of all places. They were given a fresh opportunity to live for God in a foreign land. God's plan for them, as it is for us, was to live in the world but not of the world. If we seek first Christ's kingdom and his righteousness, God will take care of the future (Matt.6:33).

Fourth, God's plan challenges us to pray and work for the good of others. The prophet who was told by the Lord at various times *not* to pray for his own people wrote to the exiles on behalf of the Lord saying, "Seek the peace and prosperity of the city to which I have carried you into exile. Pray to the Lord for it, because if it prospers, you too will prosper" (29:7). This is remarkable counsel because it was given to a people who were far more inclined to hate their captors than pray for them. Normally, oppressed people define their identity in opposition to the culture that exploits them, but in this case, Jeremiah exhorted them to do what Jesus told his disciples to do, "love your enemies and pray for those who persecute you" (Matt.5:44). They were to love their neighbors as themselves (Matt.22:39).

Jeremiah's counsel, given about 600 years before Christ, gave the people of God a hint of the Gospel ethic to come. The apostle Peter wrote, "Slaves submit yourselves to your master with all respect, not only to those who are good and considerate, but also to those who are harsh. For it is commendable if a person bears up under the pain of unjust suffering because he is conscious of God" (1 Pet.2:18-19). Jeremiah's understanding of the plan of God echoes the divine the principle that says, "Identify yourself with my interest in other people, don't identify me with your interest in other people."

Fifth, God's plan resists deception, especially the strong tendency to deceive ourselves. In his letter, Jeremiah issued an emphatic warning, "'Yes, this is what the Lord Almighty, the God of Israel, says: Do not let the prophets and diviners among you deceive you. Do not listen to the dreams you encourage them to have. They are prophesying lies to you in my name. I have not sent them,' declares the Lord" (29:8-9). By now we are used to this often repeated warning from Jeremiah. He knew that the redemptive plan of God would come under attack by leaders who thought they were doing God and the people a favor. In the name of popular spirituality, religious pluralism, civil religion and national pride, self-designated prophets in Jerusalem and Babylon predicted a short exile and a quick return to the homeland. They insisted on an up-beat, pragmatic message that they thought would encourage the people, but Jeremiah insisted on seeing the captivity for what it was and enduring it by God's grace. The false prophets were preaching independence from Babylon and Jeremiah was preaching dependence upon God. They refused to come to terms with Judah's sin while Jeremiah insisted that the exile was really God's grace in disguise. Ironically, Jeremiah warned them not to listen to the dreams they encouraged the prophets to have. The people may have deserved the prophets they got but they were not the prophets they needed. They needed teachers who would "preach the Word," teachers who would "be prepared in season and out of season," to "correct, rebuke and encourage—with great patience and careful instruction." To express Jeremiah's thought in the apostle Paul's words, Jeremiah warned them against gathering around them "a great number of teachers to say what their itching ears want to hear" (2 Tim.4:2-3). Jeremiah knew that when we take ourselves and our culture as the basic and authoritative text for making decisions and living life we are bound to fail. The temptation to exegete our hopes and dreams, as a primary sacred text with a little biblical terminology and spiritualized self-help thrown in, is always a recipe for failure.

Sixth, God's plan is fulfilled in an abiding, intimate relationship with God. The purpose of God's will is not something that lends itself to being purpose-driven or achievement oriented. It is not about stages of moral development or rounding the bases of spiritual achievement. There is no spiritual score card in God's plan for your life. Knowing God's plan for your life is all about knowing God. Jeremiah described how we would know that we are in God's will in relational terms: "'Then you will call upon me and come and pray to me, and I will listen to you. You will seek me and find me when you seek me with all your heart. I will be found by you,' declares the Lord, 'and will bring you back from captivity'" (29:12-14). The sign of knowing God's plan is not material wealth or career success or the perfect family, but an authentic, whole-hearted communion with God. Jesus used the imagery of the vine and the branches to describe what it meant to know God's will: "I am the vine; you are the branches. If you remain in me and I in you, you will bear much fruit; apart from me you can do nothing" (John 15:5). The apostle Paul described knowing God's plan this way, "I consider everything a loss compared to the surpassing greatness of knowing Christ Jesus my Lord, for whose sake I have lost all things... I want to know Christ and the power of his resurrection and the fellowship of sharing in his sufferings, becoming like him in his death, and so, somehow, to attain to the resurrection from the dead" (Phil.3:8-11).

Seventh, God's plan provokes serious opposition from those who claim to follow God. Shemaiah was one of the false prophets in Babylon who took it upon himself to start a letter campaign against Jeremiah. He sent letters to the priests in Jerusalem reprimanding them for their failure to fulfill their God-given responsibility to "put any madman who acts like a prophet into the stocks and leg-irons" (29:26). He was specifically referring to Jeremiah. "So why haven't you done anything about muzzling Jeremiah of Anathoth, who's going around posing as a prophet? He's gone so far as to write to us in Babylon, 'It's going to be a long exile, so build houses and make yourselves at home. Plant gardens and prepare Babylonian recipes" (29:27-28; The Message).

What is surprising is that after decades of unflinching spiritual integrity, courageous ministry, and fulfilled prophesy, Jeremiah could still be accused of being a madman. But then hasn't this always been the case for those who live their lives true to God's great Salvation History story? This is the story within the story for those who believe in the plan of God. The list is long of those who were thought to be either mad or spiritual posers. Noah, Joseph, Job and Moses belong alongside Jeremiah on this list of falsely accused. The supreme example is Jesus who was considered crazy by his family and called a son of the Devil by the religious leaders. Paul was beaten within an inch of his life for alleged blasphemy and Stephen was stoned to death. God's plan has never gone over well with those who refuse to listen to the Word of the Lord and insist on their own visions and dreams of how religion should succeed. God's plan to give us hope and a future invariably runs counter to popular spirituality, God-and-country religion, and self-centered visions.

7. The Gospel Covenant

"'This is the covenant I will make with the house of Israel after that time,' declares the Lord. 'I will put my law in their minds and write it on their hearts. I will be their God, and they will be my people. No longer will anyone teach his neighbor, or anyone his brother, saying, 'Know the Lord,' because they will all know me, from the least of them to the greatest,' declares the Lord. 'For I will forgive their wickedness and will remember their sins no more.'" Jeremiah 31:33-34

The trajectory of Jeremiah's prophecy leads right to the New Testament Church, the coming Kingdom of God, and the promise of everlasting life under the rule of God. The meaning and fulfillment of the New Covenant has everything to do with *who* is included in "the house of Israel." The Lord's promise, "I will make the descendants of David my servant and the Levites who minister before me as countless as the stars of the sky and as measureless as the sand on the seashore" (33:22), finds its fulfillment among both Jews and Gentiles. The remnant was not exclusively Jewish but inclusive of "all the Gentiles who bear my name"

(Acts 15:17; see Amos 9:11-12; Rom.11:5). What Jeremiah anticipated was fulfilled in the gospel of Christ which the apostle Paul described as "the power of God for the salvation of everyone who believes: first for the Jew, then for the Gentile" (Rom.1:16).

Jeremiah's stress on an essential internal transformation or a "circumcision of the heart" (4:4) was confirmed by Paul when he wrote, "A person is not a Jew who is one only outwardly, nor is circumcision merely outward and physical. No, a person is a Jew who is one inwardly; and circumcision is circumcision of the heart, by the Spirit, not by the written code. Such a person's praise is not from other people, but from God" (Rom.2:28-29). "If you belong to Christ," Paul wrote, "then you are Abraham's seed, and heirs according to the promise" (Gal.3:29). Those who are in Christ have put off their old self, which was defined in earthly categories of sin and separation, and put on a new self, "which is being renewed in knowledge in the image of its Creator. Here there is no Greek or Jew, circumcised or uncircumcised, barbarian, Scythian, slave or free, but Christ is all, and is in all" (Col.3:10-11).

A New Day Is Dawning

If Jeremiah is a parable of Jesus, then Israel is a parable of the church. The inclusiveness of the gospel rests on God's particular use of Israel. In God's unfolding plan of redemption the divine promise made to Abraham that "all peoples on earth will be blessed through you" (Gen.12:3) identified Israel as God's chosen instrument through which to bless the world. Yahweh did not choose Israel because she was either impressive or righteous (Deut.7:7; 9:4). On the contrary, among the nations she was a small, weak, inconsequential nation, but that only served to highlight the love of God that showered his affection on an easily overlooked, if not despised nation. Yahweh set his affection on Israel in order to illustrate his merciful redemption, implement his righteous commands, and impart his vision for salvation. It was a matter of exclusivity for the sake of inclusivity in order that the world might know the love of the living God.

In the history of redemption, Israel served several critical purposes.

First, she demonstrated that the object of God's mercy and love was not based on merit or achievement, but on God's grace. There was no room for boasting and no place for pride. Jeremiah expressed human need succinctly when he said, "The heart is deceitful above all things and beyond cure. Who can understand it?" (17:9).

Second, Israel illustrated the failure of external religion to transform people. Even though she had received the best external religious system available, she had wilfully chosen to go her own rebellious way, so that at times she was condemned as being even worse than her pagan neighbors. "All of us have become like one who is unclean," wrote Isaiah, "and all our righteous acts are like filthy rags" (Isa.64:6).

Third, Israel was God's chosen people through whom the Anointed One was to come. This expectation of the Messiah emerged slowly over the course of Salvation History and it wasn't until Jesus came that the various pictures of the Messiah as Conquering King and Suffering Servant converged into one person. Israel never set out to be the object of God's mercy, the paradigm of religious failure and the line of descent for the Messiah. There has always been an unexpected hiddenness in God's providential plan that inherently resists human pride and manipulation and points to the cross and resurrection of Jesus Christ.

The climax of Jeremiah's prophecy causes us to think of Jesus Christ from the time of his coming (31:15; Matt.2:18) to the time of his rule (33:15-17; Heb.12:2). Every dimension of salvation that Jeremiah foresaw under the New Covenant depended on the risen Lord Jesus Christ for its fulfillment. Jeremiah's poetic description of judgment and salvation provides a vivid description of our experience of repentance and redemption and corresponds to what it means to be "born again" in Christ.

Throughout this section, known as the "book of consolation," Jeremiah looks forward to a coming day when the people of God will be restored to the promised land, to good health and to the fortunes of Jacob. Phrases such as "the days are coming," and "in that day" serve as a refrain throughout this passage announcing the future certainty of the benefits of judgment and the blessing of salvation (30:3,8; 31:1,26,31). Jeremiah's Spirit-led vision of a re-united Israel and Judah is a picture of that day, *now present*, when "the dividing wall of hostility" between Jews and Gentiles is brought down because of Christ who preaches peace to both those who are near and those who are far away (Eph.2:14-17).

Terror on Every Side

However, according to Jeremiah, the process leading up to that day involved an unnaturally long and painful ordeal. He used powerful metaphors to illustrate people's fear and terror. Once self-reliant, strong men would be like women in labor, bent over in pain, with their pale faces contorted in agony, enduring one of the worst days of their lives (30:6). They would be like slaves subjugated by foreign oppressors, or exiles driven from their homeland, or terminally ill patients without hope (30:8,10,12). They would be like the poor without an advocate or a people without allies, or outcasts without a defender. And the sad fact would be that their awful pain, terrible social bondage, and physical demise could not be blamed on anyone other than themselves.

Jeremiah captured the essence of this experience in his first line, "Cries of fear are heard–terror, not peace" (30:5). He gave the reporters of his time a sound-bite that summed up the feeling of suffering and doom that pervaded Judah's culture. It is also a fitting tag line to describe the modern era and American culture. People today wrestle with deep feelings of personal insignificance and live with a constant pressure of trying to make something of themselves. The question of meaning is often met on the surface with cynicism and in the soul with despair. The question of God is usually reduced to a matter of personal preference and sentiment. The one remaining issue of enduring concern seems to be the question of happiness. Yet even this quest for personal peace and pleasure is dealt with in the most superficial ways.

Our culture's "eat, drink, and be merry, for tomorrow we die" philosophy of life seems to have met its match in a series of world events since 9/11. Devastating tsunamis, two costly wars, a global economic recession, the resurgence of AIDs and the threat of a flu pandemic compel us to re-examine the meaning and vulnerability of life, the purpose of history, the forces of evil, the limits of human power, the pursuit of justice, and most importantly our relationship to God. We might like nothing better than to tell ourselves that it was all a bad dream and we can go back to bed, pull the blanket of self-preoccupation over our heads and go back to sleep. But in momentous times we are challenged to look beyond ourselves and to examine issues greater than our personal peace and pleasure.

For Jeremiah, the message of judgment, captured in his phrase, "terror on every side," was meant to awaken Judah from her dogmatic slumbers, her religion-as-usual, her popular spiritualities, her obsession with idols, sex, and self, in order that she might turn to the Lord. The false prophets could no longer get away with saying, "the temple of the Lord, the temple of the Lord, the temple of the Lord." They couldn't claim "Peace, peace!" because there was no peace. The parallels between Jeremiah's day and our own are powerful. The cries of fear are heard–terror not peace is the order of the day. People are empty, confused, and broken. The collapse of the World Trade Center because of an unforeseen and unimaginable terrorist attack symbolizes the vulnerability of our culture to human hate. And in spite of all the government's effort to assure our safety, we are confronted with the fact that there is no guarantee for safety in the world. In a world that believes in the survival of the fittest, in everyone doing what is right in their own eyes and in the validity of all religions, terrorism has dramatically reminded us that there is a difference between good and evil, right and wrong, justice and injustice. Because of evil regimes and terrorism, humankind is forced to recognize moral limits and respond to their violation.

The Space Shuttle Columbia's catastrophic disaster in 2003 painfully confronts us with the limits of our technology, the frailty of our finitude, and reminds us once again that our destiny and our future does not lie in space. It is one thing to accept the risks and explore the Creator's cosmic wasteland with its austere beauty and mind boggling dimensions, but it is another to look to space for meaning and purpose. Nature serves to inspire and humble, but it must never be allowed to become a rival god that offers false hope to sinful humankind. No matter how advanced we become in our scientific technology we cannot avert disasters. In spite of great advances in the medical sciences we cannot prevent an outbreak of a disease such as SARS or the H1N1 flu pandemic. The Bible teaches that sin separates us from God, from one another, from nature, and from ourselves. We are reminded that no place is safe and that our salvation is not found in health.

With his warning of "terror on every side" Jeremiah captured the multi-dimensional tragedy of evil. His graphic metaphors of sin and evil were not intended to depress people or to entertain them. Jeremiah's purpose was redemptive. His hope was that a true grasp of our fallen human condition and a sinful world would cause people to turn to God for forgiveness and salvation. As sinners we need to turn to God in repentance. As victims of sin we need to turn to God for rescue. Either way, and it is always both, we were meant to seek God, who is our only hope for security and salvation. Jeremiah promised that the redemptive purposes of God's judgment would become evident in time: "The storm of the Lord will burst out in wrath," and "the fierce anger of the Lord will not turn back until he fully accomplishes the purposes of his heart. In days to come you will understand this" (30:23-24).

The Joy of Salvation

Jeremiah contrasted these images of judgment and descriptive metaphors of evil with an even more powerful and compelling picture of salvation. He prophesied that a new day was coming when the yoke of oppression would be broken (30:8), old wounds would be healed (30:17), the city would be rebuilt and songs of thanksgiving would be heard in her streets (30:18-19). "Their leader will be one of their own;" Jeremiah prophesied, "their ruler will arise from among them" (30:21). Jeremiah's messianic prophecies appear more subtle than the prophet Isaiah's but no less significant and his vision of a reunited Israel finds its fulfillment in the Body of Christ. "'At that time,' declares the Lord, 'I will be the God of all the clans of Israel, and they will be my people.'" (31:1). Jeremiah's prophecy corresponds with the apostle Peter's description of the Church as "a chosen people, a royal priesthood, a holy nation, a people belonging to God." What Jeremiah promised, Peter proclaimed, "Once you were not a people, but now you are the people of God; once you had not received mercy, but now you have received mercy" (1 Peter 2:9-10). Jeremiah's endearing description of Virgin Israel corresponds to the apostle Paul's picture of the Bride of Christ (31:4; Eph.5:25-27) and Jacob's song of praise among the nations parallels Christ's great commission to "go and make disciples of all nations..." (31:7; Matt.28:19).

Although Jeremiah is better known as the weeping prophet, he described the joy of salvation in vivid social and pastoral images. He prophesied that mourning would cease and there would be dancing in the streets: "You will take up your tambourines and go out to dance with the joyful." "...Maidens will dance and be glad, young men and old as well. I will turn their mourning into gladness; I will give them comfort and joy instead of sorrow" (31:4, 13). Lush vineyards on the hills of Samaria were beyond any exiled Jerusalemite's imagination, but it was Jeremiah's way of saying that a new day was coming. "For the Lord will ransom Jacob and redeem them from the hand of those stronger than they. They will come and shout for joy on the heights of Zion; they will rejoice in the bounty of the Lord—the grain, the new wine and the oil, the young of the flocks and herds. They will be like a well-watered garden, and they will sorrow no more" (31:11-12).

These social and pastoral images of salvation find their fulfillment in the New Testament description of Christ's coming. When John the Baptist introduced Jesus he was "full of joy" because he heard the bridegroom's voice (John 3:29). It was John's way of saying, "Let the celebration begin!" Jesus commenced his public ministry by announcing "the year of the Lord's favor" (Luke 4:19). He healed the sick, restored sight to the blind, and preached good news to the poor. He changed water to wine at the wedding feast in Cana of Galilee. He removed people's heavy burdens in exchange for an easy yoke. He fed the multitude and raised the dead. Jesus' actions signaled the fulfillment of Jeremiah's prophecy. The celebration had begun and even though many refused to enter into this joy, the fact was undeniable, a new day had dawn (Matt.11:16).

The apostle Paul resonated with Jeremiah's pastoral imagery of salvation when he spoke of the fruit of the Spirit (Gal.5:22) and the "fruit of the light" which consists "in all goodness, righteousness and truth" (Eph.5:9). Paul transposed Jeremiah's pastoral description of the land, into a character description of the person in Christ. What is crucial is that we make the connection between Jeremiah's prophecy and Christ's coming. Jeremiah's picture of a reunited Israel gathered from distant nations, celebrating joyfully and experiencing abundance, is a picture of the Gospel evangelizing the nations and transforming lives.

Jeremiah gave his message of hope and consolation well aware that God's plan of redemption involved both suffering and confession. It was clear to him that God's salvation would one day overcome this history of suffering and wipe away the tears. What was unclear to Jeremiah, as well as to all the prophets, was to what extent God would identify with human suffering and demonstrate his compassion for his prodigal people. Jeremiah interrupted his positive message of celebration unexpectedly with the sound of weeping. "A voice is heard in Ramah, mourning and great weeping, Rachel weeping for her children and refusing to be comforted, because her children are no more" (31:15). Jeremiah captured the pathos of Israel's suffering by recalling Rachel's grief at Ramah, where she died giving birth to a son (Gen.35:16-20). Jeremiah associated this event and this site, which was some five miles north of Jerusalem near Bethlehem, with the place where the captives were gathered before being "carried into exile to Babylon" (40:1). The weeping could be heard in Ramah through the centuries from Rachel in labor to the exiles being deported. It seemed like one long tragic history of grief. But Jeremiah was not the only one to use Ramah and Rachel's weeping as a type. Matthew connected Jeremiah's prophesy to Herod's massacre of innocent boys in Bethlehem following the birth of Jesus (Matt.2:17-18). He understood that the birth of Jesus was crucial to overcoming this history of suffering and sorrow.

We sense that Jeremiah was delighted to say, "Restrain your voice from weeping and your eyes from tears..." (31:16). A new day was coming when the people of God would be empowered to return to the Lord with their whole heart. As opposed to the meaningless confessions that Jeremiah had previously recorded (14:7-9) and the suggested confessions that the people should have prayed (3:22-25; 14:19-22) this confession was authentic and came from the heart. Each one meant it when they said, "You disciplined me like an unruly calf, and I have been disciplined. Restore me, and I will return, because you are the Lord my God.

After I strayed, I repented; after I came to understand, I beat my breast. I was ashamed and humiliated because I bore the disgrace of my youth" (31:18-19). Yahweh was eager and ready to respond to such a confession: "'Is not Ephraim my dear son, the child in whom I delight? Though I often speak against him, I still remember him. Therefore my heart yearns for him; I have great compassion for him,' declares the Lord" (31:20).

Jeremiah's description of God's compassion makes us think of the waiting Father in the parable of the lost son. God is so ready to embrace his son, who is lost in the far country, that he wants road signs and guideposts put up to clearly mark the way home (31:21). Jeremiah likens Israel first to a lost son and then to an unfaithful daughter, but the point is the same, Yahweh's message is filled with compassion, "Return, O Virgin Israel....How long will you wander, O unfaithful daughter?" (31:22-23). It is difficult to know how far to take the enigmatic promise, "The Lord will create a new thing on earth—a woman will surround a man," but according to Old Testament scholar R. K. Harrison the possibilities point in the direction of the Incarnation. "The innovation of a woman protecting a man describes the loving care with which a physically weaker partner surrounds and sustains the stronger one. In the New Covenant the Lord descends to the level of his people, limiting Himself to the point where they can lay hold upon Him. This situation is described in Christ's incarnation by the phrase 'the Word became flesh' (John 1:14), where God became what we are in order to make us what He Himself is."[xix] In contrast to Jeremiah's nightmarish visions of judgment, this vision of salvation refreshed the weary and satisfied the faint and filled the prophet with a pleasant feeling (31:25-26). It was one vision that he must have wished he didn't have to wake up from.

The New Covenant was by no means new to God. Everything in the Mosaic covenant pointed forward to this New Covenant. The essence of being God's covenant people was never a matter of external religion, ethnic identity, ritual conformity and legalistic duty. The New Covenant was not new in the sense that over time God came up with a better plan. Jeremiah was not introducing a new improved program that promised to work better. God's promises through Adam, Noah, Abraham, Moses, and David, all pointed forward to a personal relationship with God based on God's love and mercy. What was new was that God was making the means and the power of his redemptive purposes more fully known. That which was hidden was being revealed, but even then Jeremiah's prophesy did not make full disclosure of what would only be revealed when Christ came (Eph.1:9-10).

"The time is coming," announced Jeremiah, when the experience of judgment, so vitally important in making people aware of their sin and need for God, will be superseded by the good news of salvation. "'Just as I watched over them to uproot and tear down, and to overthrow, destroy and bring disaster, so I will watch over them to build and to plant,' declares the Lord" (31:28). The defeatism of the past will no longer dominate human minds and the religious excuses, instigated by works righteousness, will be seen for what they are, hollow and empty. The New Covenant will underscore personal accountability, a truth that has never lacked emphasis in the Word of God, but one that has often been obscured by religion-as-usual. The New Covenant will make it impossible for people to blame others for their faithlessness. "In those days people will no longer say, 'The fathers have eaten sour grapes, and the children's teeth are set on edge.' Instead, everyone will die for his own sin; whoever eats sour grapes—his own teeth will be set on edge" (31:29-30).

The Gospel makes it illegitimate for people to use their ethnicity or the religion of their parents or their cultural backgrounds as an excuse for rejecting God's provision of salvation. God's way of redemption would no longer be hidden in Israel or expressed in a sacrificial system but witnessed throughout the world by the Spirit of Christ. The old covenant was like an arranged marriage with one loving partner and another who acted imposed upon and wanted out of the relationship. In that arrangement, as we have seen, God was the jilted lover and Israel the adulteress. "'They broke my covenant, though I was a husband to them,' declares the Lord" (31:32). By contrast the New Covenant is deeply personal and based on mutual love. God still takes the initiative, but this time the relationship is strengthened from the inside-out and is based on forgiveness. Knowing God is no longer based on external conformity and religious performance. Under the New Covenant, God goes beyond laying down expectations and instead, by his grace, transforms our whole internal disposition. This indwelling principle based on God's presence and forgiveness leads to a personal relationship with the living God.

> "'This is the covenant I will make with the house of Israel after that time,' declares the Lord. 'I will put my law in their minds and write it on their hearts. I will be their God, and they will be my people. No longer will a man teach his neighbor, or a man his brother, saying, 'Know the Lord,' because they will all know me, from the least of them to the greatest,' declares the Lord. 'For I will forgive their

wickedness and will remember their sins no
more.'" (31:33-34).

Jeremiah did not attempt to explain how God planned
to do this, but there was no doubt in his mind that "he who
appoints the sun to shine by day, who decrees the moon and
stars to shine by night, who stirs up the sea so that its waves
roar" would accomplish his will (31:35-37). There was more
to the meaning and mystery of the New Covenant than
Jeremiah prophesied, but it was clear that its fulfillment was
tied to the coming of the Anointed One, "a righteous
Branch sprout from David's line" (33:15; see 23:5; 30:9).
Jeremiah promised that the coming ruler would arise from
their own ranks and his intimacy with Yahweh would be
unparalleled (30:21). Beyond this, nothing more specific was
known about the New Covenant until Jesus came. But in
Jesus the means of implementing the New Covenant became
powerfully clear. The prophecy of Jeremiah and the passion
of Christ were inseparably linked. In the upper room, Jesus
told his disciples, "This cup is the New Covenant in my
blood, which is poured out for you" (Luke 22:20; 1
Cor.11:25). In that moment the means of forgiveness and
the power of the indwelling principle were revealed. As the
author of Hebrews asserted, "...Christ is the mediator of a
New Covenant, that those who are called may receive the
promised eternal inheritance—now that he has died as a
ransom to set them free from the sins committed under the
first covenant" (Heb.9:15).

The New Covenant was revealed in Jesus' conversation
with Nicodemus, when he said, "You should not be surprised
at my saying, 'You must be born again.' The wind blows
wherever it pleases. You hear its sound, but you cannot tell
where it comes from or where it is going. So it is with

everyone born of the Spirit" (John 3:7-8). Jesus pictured the power of the New Covenant when he used the imagery of the vine and branches. "Remain in me, and I will remain in you. No branch can bear fruit by itself; it must remain in the vine. Neither can you bear fruit unless you remain in me...If you remain in me and my words remain in you, ask whatever you wish, and it will be given you" (John 15:4, 7).

The apostle Paul equated the indwelling principle of the New Covenant with being in Christ, "If anyone is in Christ, he is a new creation; the old has gone, the new has come!" (2 Cor.5:17). Instead of being conformed to the world, Christ's followers are to "be transformed by the renewing of [their] mind" (Rom.12:2). Paul laid out the theology of the New Covenant when he spoke of "the glorious riches of this mystery, which is Christ in you, the hope of glory" (Col.1:27). This is why he said that Christ "has made us competent as ministers of a New Covenant—not of the letter but of the Spirit; for the letter kills, but the Spirit gives life" (2 Cor.3:6).

Jeremiah's message helps us understand our captivity—our bondage to sin and death. His images of salvation offer us a vision of the gift of salvation—our liberation from sin and death. And the promise of the New Covenant points directly to the means of that redemption—the cross and resurrection of Jesus Christ. The apostle Paul recalled the words that Jesus used when he established the Lord's Supper, "This cup is the New Covenant in my blood; do this, whenever you drink it, in remembrance of me." Then he added, "For whenever you eat this bread and drink this cup, you proclaim the Lord's death until he comes" (1 Cor.11:25-26). The complete fulfillment of Jeremiah's prophecy remains outstanding, but the means of that fulfillment has been clearly revealed. The dividing line in history is not between *eras*, ancient and modern, but between *epics*, redemptive and heroic. The choice is between God's Salvation History and our own personal quest for significance. We either embrace this New Covenant as a gift from God that leads to everlasting life or we insist on our own way that leads inevitably to everlasting death.

8. Rejecting Renewal

"We will not listen to the message
you have spoken to us in the name
of the Lord!"
Jeremiah 44:16

It was not Jeremiah's fault that the gospel of hope fell on deaf ears. His reputation as the weeping prophet stemmed not from his personality, which I doubt was melancholy, but from the people who remained doggedly resistant to the Word of the Lord throughout his long ministry. Jeremiah was not by nature an uptight, downcast individual who needed positive feedback to function. If anything he was a flinty, square-jawed prophet who refused to give in or give up. He delivered the Word of the Lord straight-up, without equivocation or compromise.

As we have said, the highpoint of the book of Jeremiah comes with the description of the New Covenant and the promise of restoration. The two sections that follow bring the book to completion. In chapters 34-45, various incidents are described that illustrate Judah's stubborn refusal to follow the Word of the Lord. In chapters 46-51, we have a compilation of Jeremiah's messages of judgment against the surrounding nations. The historical appendix (52:1-34) concludes both sections by describing the fall of Jerusalem and is also found in 39:1-14 and in 2 Kings 25:1-30.

Case Studies of Rejection

What appears at first to be a miscellaneous collection of unrelated incidents is actually a careful study in blatant, inexcusable rejection of God's will for his people. The chronology of events is not nearly as important as the chronicle of stubborn, hard-hearted resistance to the Word of the Lord. There appears to be a parallel pattern in the presentation of cases that reinforces the message.

(1) Zedekiah presides over the Broken Covenant (34:8-22)	(4) Zedekiah's false appeal for spiritual direction (37:1-38:28)
(2) The Recabites and simple obedience (35:1-19)	(5) Gedaliah's obedience without vigilance against evil (40:1-41:17)
(3) Jehoiakim burns the scroll (36:1-32)	(6) Johanan and people reject the Word of the Lord (42:1-43:13) (7) The people embrace pagan practices in Egypt (44:1-30)

Picture a prosecutor systematically laying out his evidence for a conviction. These historical episodes are Jeremiah's case studies. They boldly demonstrate the forbearance of God's grace and the necessity of divine judgment. They make the case for God's righteous justice and the need for judgment. In any era, including our own, these case studies in disobedience provide a wake-up call for the people who profess to follow the risen Lord Jesus

Christ. There is no secret to true spiritual renewal. It consists of true freedom, basic obedience, sensitivity to the Word of God and openness to God's will. It means vigilance against evil, living by faith instead of fear and practicing the true spiritual disciplines. This may sound like a tall order, but the cost of *not* following the Lord God is always greater than the cost of simple, whole-hearted obedience.

Seven Signs of Spiritual Renewal

The keys to spiritual renewal are no mystery and the path of obedience is not nearly as complicated as it is often made out to be. It is not that difficult to understand what God wants from us. In fact, it often takes considerable effort, along with willful self-deception and wrong-headed activism to resist the will of God. In the seven cases presented by Jeremiah the people were *blessed* with clear, unambiguous spiritual direction. They knew the will of God, but Israel chose to do the opposite. The strategies of self-deception, plus the rationalization of power and the motivation of fear, proved to be much more complex than the straightforward will of God. Each case alerts professing believers to the deceptive nature of spirituality. There was a great deal of discussion among the people and the leaders about covenant-keeping, fasting, intercessory prayer, and the will of God, but all of this "spirituality" amounted to only a religious performance. It was a thinly veiled spiritual veneer covering up selfishness, willful resistance to God's will and worldly strategies of self-preservation. These seven negative case studies warn us of some of the obvious pitfalls on the path to obedience. A careful study of them yields seven positive signs of spiritual renewal. Although the people of God failed miserably, their negative example can become an incentive and a guide to spiritual renewal. Jeremiah's chronicle becomes an important advisory to all those who are serious about building up the Body of Christ today.

Spiritual renewal works for social justice (34:8-22).

Under pressure from Nebuchadnezzar's besieging army in 587 B.C., King Zedekiah did something right. He led the people in a solemn covenant to emancipate the Hebrew slaves (34:1-22). Apparently the crisis of Babylon's pending invasion produced a crisis of royal conscience and a last ditch effort to win God's favor. Jerusalem's leaders made a public appeal to God. They invoked the divine name, quoted the divine law, and performed a public ritual to solemnize their vow. In a show of corporate solidarity, they solemnly cut a calf in two and the covenant signers walked between the two pieces. The rite signified that anyone who reneged on the covenant would suffer the same fate as the calf (34:18; see Gen.15:10, 17).

The leadership elite, the socially privileged and the economically well off agreed to set their Hebrew slaves free. One can only imagine the joy that these liberated slaves felt, their financial indebtedness forgiven and their freedom regained. However their feeling of elation was only temporary. They were no sooner released, when the Babylonian army withdrew, the imminence of the crisis passed, and the leadership had a sudden and pernicious change of heart. The brevity of the narrative description is in itself telling. It simply reads, "They agreed, and set them free. But afterward they changed their minds and took back the slaves they had freed and enslaved them again" (34:10-11). The narrative implies that their immoral reversal was as easy as flipping a coin.

The ease with which the leadership elite broke their covenant testifies to the duplicity of their motives, the intractable nature of social evil and the power of a social class to reinforce injustice. They knew all along that the Lord commanded the release of their Hebrew slaves, but they refused to obey the biblical commands until disaster bore down on them. Their "tit-for-tat" quid-pro-quo morality was blatantly self-serving. And as soon as they got what they wanted, the power of group-think took over and their pragmatic economic logic kicked in and persuaded them to go back to the way things were. Undoubtedly they felt they had good, sensible reasons for maintaining their social status quo.

The incident testifies to human nature's inherent moral insensitivity and the tendency to do only that which pacifies the conscience and serves individual self-interests. As was true of Jerusalem's ruling elite, the impulse to do good is often not based on heart righteousness and a desire to obey God, but on the feelings of the moment, a desire to look good before others, and an attempt to gain favor with God.

We may have come to Christ out of a personal desire to quell a disturbed spirit, to satisfy a restless longing in our soul for God, or to experience an inner peace that we knew was missing. However in coming to Christ we have discovered that the Christian Faith does not stop with inner peace or a private faith. John Wesley rightly held that "Christianity is essentially a social religion; and that to turn it into a solitary religion, is indeed to destroy it."xx Jesus leads us into the real world of work and family and society for the sake of Christ and His Kingdom. He tells us to take up our cross and follow Him. Jesus calls us to follow him into our Jerusalem, into our families, work places, and schools, with the soul-saving, life-transforming gospel. The Christian's personal faith was meant to have public impact everywhere, from our home life to the marketplace. And the challenge to make disciples and set things right is extended to the ends of the earth.

There is no secluded place for a private, individualized, spiritualized religious faith that lets *me* focus on *my* self and *my* religious tastes and spiritual preferences. Jesus says, "Come follow me," and we know that he is heading toward the Cross. This is why Jesus said, "Do not suppose that I have come to bring peace to the earth. I did not come to bring peace, but a sword. For I have come to turn 'a man against his father, a daughter against her mother, a daughter-in-law against her mother-in-law—a man's enemies will be the members of his own household'" (Matt. 10:35). This is disturbing news for people who thought Christ would simply make life go better. There is far more to following Christ than we bargained for. "Whoever finds his life will lose it, and whoever loses his life for my sake will find it" (Matt.10:39).

Ron Sider's clarion call for social justice in the 1970s, entitled, *Rich Christians in an Age of Hunger*, could be re-titled today, *Rich Christians in an Age of Hungry Christians*, because many who are suffering famine and persecution around the world are our brothers and sisters in Christ. As the Body of Christ has grown so has our social responsibility. The meaning of Paul's warning shatters our complacency: "For anyone who eats and drinks without recognizing the body of the Lord eats and drinks judgment on himself" (1 Cor.11:29). True spiritual renewal is not simply an inward disposition, a certain attitude, or a pious feeling, but a living sacrifice of all we are to Christ. This kind of offering could only be done by the grace and mercy of Christ. Our commitment to Christ is grandly inclusive of all we are and have. Thus, we can no longer live according to the self-serving pragmatism of the world. We were meant to live transformed lives. We were meant to live today in the light of the coming Kingdom of Christ. This is why Jesus said, "Seek first his kingdom and his righteousness" (Matt.6:33).

In the tradition of Jesus' teaching in the Sermon on the Mount, Paul gives a comprehensive picture of Agape love— Christian love (Rom.12:9-21). "Love must be sincere." Literally, without hypocrisy. Authentic love is not a performance, nor is it a sentiment. "Hate what is evil." "Love's hatred of evil expresses an aversion, an abhorrence, even a 'loathing', while love's clinging to what is good expresses a sticking or bonding as if with glue."[xxi] Love is measured inversely according to the degree to which we hate evil. "Love is therefore both sweet and bitter. It can yield; but it can also be harsh. It can preserve peace; but it can also engage in conflict...Only the love which is strong enough to abhor that which is evil can cleave to that which is good. Love forgets–and knows; forgives—and punishes; freely receives—and utterly rejects."[xxii] Paul adds to this love, affection and honor. "Be devoted to one another in brotherly love. Honor one another above yourselves. Never be lacking in zeal, but keep your spiritual fervor, serving the Lord." Each of Paul's bullet points could trigger endless debate, legal qualifications, special nuances, and excuses, but Paul is not talking to people who are trying to make a deal with God. Paul is not presenting the terms of a contract. Agape love is the do-whatever-it-takes love of self-sacrifice. It is the opposite of a self-serving, what's in it for me, self-love. As James put it, "So then, if you know the good you ought to do and don't do it, you sin" (James 4:17).

Spiritual renewal practices simple obedience (35:1-19).

If for no other reason than Jeremiah's persistent ministry, Jerusalem's leaders had no excuse for breaking their covenant with God and the people. For decades Jeremiah had made the case for biblical obedience in a variety of effective ways. One of his unforgettable object-lessons involved the Recabites, a large extended family who had vowed not to drink wine, build homes or farm. They were committed to living in tents and grazing their cattle on the open range ever since their forefather, Jonadab, had pledged himself and his descendants to a nomadic way of life. For two and half centuries they had been resident aliens engaged in an austere effort to avoid social corruption.

Twelve years before the siege of Jerusalem and the episode of the broken covenant, during the reign of Jehoiakim (ca 601 BC), Jeremiah went to elaborate lengths to make a case for obedience. He was led by the Lord to set up the Recabites in a compromising situation. The Recabites had been forced to seek shelter in Jerusalem because of the Babylonian invasion (35:11). One could say that they had been forced into urban exile.

Jeremiah's invitation to the Recabites to attend a reception in the temple must have come as a surprise. They were certainly not on anyone's social list nor were they held in high regard. In fact it is more than likely that these country nomads were recipients of charity and were looked down upon by the ruling elite in Jerusalem. When they were ushered into a special room, they must have wondered why. Important temple officials were in attendance and an abundant supply of wine made the occasion feel not only hospitable, but auspicious. It appears that Jeremiah had done everything he could think of to tempt these Recabites in urban exile to accept his toast and follow his invitation to "drink some wine" (35:5).

But together they made a united stand, saying, "We do not drink wine, because our forefather Jonadab son of Recab gave us this command..." (35:6). In spite of all the social pressure Jeremiah had managed to exert, the Recabites calmly declined his invitation to drink the wine and used the incident and the setting to tell their story. Jeremiah must have been pleased. As he had hoped, his sting operation had failed and left him with a powerful object lesson which he immediately used as the Lord directed. His message to the people of Judah was not about wine or the nomadic lifestyle, but about simple, basic obedience to the Word of the Lord. Jeremiah asked the Lord's question, "Will you not learn a lesson and obey my words?"and then gave the Lord's verdict, "But I have spoken to you again and again, yet you have not obeyed me" (35:14). For generations the Recabites had obeyed their long-deceased forefather's one-time command, but the people of Jerusalem had not paid attention or listened to the living God's on-going revelation.

Spiritual renewal involves taking God at his word and obeying what it says. Jesus said, "If you hold to my teaching, you are really my disciples. Then you will know the truth, and the truth will set you free" (John 8:31). James warned, "Do not merely listen to the word, and so deceive yourselves. Do what it says....Those who look intently into the perfect law that gives freedom and continue in it—not forgetting what they have heard but doing it—they will be blessed in what they do" (James 1:22, 25). If people can be committed to professional oaths, fraternity pledges, legal contracts, club rules, and friendship agreements, then the followers of the risen Lord can and should be committed to obeying his commands.

Spiritual renewal takes to heart the Word of God (36:1-32).

Jeremiah traced Judah's resistance to renewal to a critical incident that took place some fifteen years before the broken covenant and around three years before the Recabite object lesson. It occurred in the fifth year of Jehoiakim's reign (605 BC) when Baruch, Jeremiah's trusted assistant, went to "the house of the Lord on a day of fasting" to read all the words of the Lord that Jeremiah had dictated to him. Baruch did just what Jeremiah asked him to do, because the prophet was banned from the temple. Baruch read the entire scroll, which may have contained much of the material found in chapters 1-25, to "all the people in Jerusalem and those who had come from the towns of Judah" (36:9).

In the audience that day was Micaiah, son of Gemariah and grandson of Shaphan. Shaphan, as you may recall was the official who read the Law of God to King Josiah (2 Kings 22:3-23:3) fifteen years earlier. Now his grandson, who apparently shared his grandfather's sensitivity to the Word of the Lord, asked Baruch to read Jeremiah's scroll again, this time to all the officials. "When they heard all these words, they looked at each other in fear and said to Baruch, 'We must report all these words to the king'" (36:16). After confirming that Jeremiah was the author of the scroll and warning Baruch to take Jeremiah and go and hide, the officials reported to King Jehoiakim what had taken place. The king immediately sent for the scroll and Jehudi read it out loud to the king. When Jehudi finished with a section, the king cut it off with a scribe's knife and threw it into the fireplace. In spite of three officials, including Gemariah, urging him not to, he systematically cut up the entire scroll and burned it. Then he ordered the arrest of Baruch the scribe and Jeremiah the prophet. "But the Lord had hidden them" (36:26).

The parallels between Josiah's hearing of the Word of the Lord and Jehoiakim shredding the Word of the Lord are striking. In each case, the Word of the Lord was read three times, first in the temple and then in the palace. When Josiah heard the Word of the Lord he tore his robes (2 Kings 22:11), but when Jehoiakim heard the Word of the Lord he tore it up (36:23). Josiah himself read the Book of the Covenant in the presence of all the people and "renewed the covenant in the presence of the Lord" (2 Kings 23:3), but Jehoiakim sought to the destroy the word and capture those who delivered it. If Jehoiakim had handled the Word of the Lord faithfully it may have been a turning point for Judah that would have led to renewal. As it was, the king's reaction emboldened the officials who despised the Word of the Lord, and discouraged those officials who might have responded obediently.

The picture we have of Jehoiakim entertaining his court officials with his brazen disrespect for the Word of the Lord is not unlike today's biblical critics who build their reputations on disparaging the Word of the Lord. They don't cut it up with a scribe's knife, they slice it up with their speculation and sophistry. Like Jehoiakim, they sit in judgment on the Word of the Lord. They "burn the scroll" and feel they can get away with it without suffering judgment, but their rejection of God's word serves only to seal their fate.

Spiritual renewal accepts the plan of God (37:1-10,16-17; 38:14-39:7).

Jeremiah's chronicle of resistance returns to King Zedikiah in order to illustrate a much less brazen rejection of God's word than Jehoiakim had displayed, but no less real and, in the end, just as devastating. Zedekiah and his attendants refused to pay any attention to the words of the Lord, but they continually sought Jeremiah's spiritual support and counsel (37:2). What is especially interesting in Zedekiah's case is that his quest for divine support and his appeal to the Lord's prophet was not for show. When he said to Jeremiah, "Please pray to the Lord our God for us," he truly meant it (37:3). His private consultations with Jeremiah and his assurances of protection confirm that he honestly wanted to know whether there was a word from the Lord (37:17). Three times in this section, we are told that Zedekiah sought the Word of the Lord through Jeremiah. "I am going to ask you something," Zedekiah said to Jeremiah. "Do not hide anything from me" (38:14). But on all three occasions, Zedekiah heard a word from the Lord that he refused to accept. He wanted a word from the Lord that preached success, not judgment. He wanted a word that was compatible with his hopes and dreams, instead he received a message that confirmed that Judah was under judgment.

One of the factors that dissuaded Zedekiah from accepting the Word of the Lord was his fear of what others thought of his authority and rule. If his secret meetings with Jeremiah proved that he was serious about knowing God's plan, they also indicated that he feared what others thought of him. For Zedekiah to accept God's word meant he would have to surrender and be perceived as a coward. Jeremiah said to the king, "This is what the Lord God Almighty, the God of Israel, says, 'If you surrender to the officers of the king of Babylon, your life will be spared and this city will not be burned down; you and your family will live. But if you will not surrender to the officers of the king of Babylon, this city will be handed over to the Babylonians and they will burn it down; your yourself will not escape from their hands'" (38:17-18). In the end, Zedekiah tried to escape, but he and his family were caught. He was forced to witness the execution of his sons before his eyes were put out and he was taken to Babylon in shackles (39:5-7).

The tragedy of Zedekiah is that he desperately wanted the will of God to conform to his expectations. He wanted the plan of God to be compatible with his vision of success. Zedekiah was like the person today who wants God to bless their hopes and dreams. Imbedded in their show of sincerity is a duplicity that refuses to accept the will of God. They may be unaware of the negative spiritual dynamics at work in their souls, because their rejection of God's will is more by default than defiance. Zedekiah was not asking, "What is God's program on earth and how do I fit in?" Instead, he was asking, "How does God fit into my life?" His demise demonstrates that "God's will is not my culture, it is not individually tailored to fit the assumptions I hold dear in life." In other words, "God's will does not ratify my present lifestyle."[xxiii] "The world and its desires pass away," wrote the apostle John, "but the person who does the will of God lives forever" (1 John 2:17).

Spiritual renewal resists evil (40:7-41:17).

In each case study presented by Jeremiah there was potential for spiritual renewal. God's blessings were evident in specific, practical ways: the law of God against slavery was proclaimed, the Recabites exemplified simple obedience, the Word of the Lord was made known publicly, and the guidance of God was given personally. Following the fall of Jerusalem in 587 B.C. Nebuchadnezzar, king of Babylon, appointed Gedaliah, Shaphan's grandson and Micaiah's cousin to be governor. Gedaliah represented God's blessing in a time of crisis. He stepped into a leadership vacuum and followed Jeremiah's counsel. He did what Zedekiah could not bring himself to do. He advised the people, "Settle down in the land and serve the king of Babylon, and it will go well with you" (40:9; 2 Kings 25:24). Gedaliah's sensible, selfless leadership brought stability to the region and encouraged many of the Jews who had fled to other countries to return to Judah. Their homecoming was marked by security and success, and we are told that "they harvested an abundance of wine and summer fruit" (40:12).

However, Gedaliah's leadership suffered a fatal flaw. He was naive about the forces of evil plotting against him. Johanan, one of the guerilla fighters still operating in the open country, came to Gedaliah at Mizpah to warn him that Baalis, king of the Ammonites, had sent Ishmael to assassinate him (40:13-14). Johanan requested permission to kill Ishmael. He reasoned with Gedaliah, saying, "Why should he take your life and cause all the Jews who are gathered around you to be scattered and the remnant of Judah to perish?" But Gedaliah refused to even consider the possibility, saying to Johanan, "Don't do such a thing! What you are saying about Ishmael is not true" (40:15-16). If Gedaliah had not so quickly dismissed the threat, but had sought the Lord's guidance and consulted with Jeremiah, he might have spared not only his life but the lives of many others (41:2-7). Gedaliah was guilty of wanting to believe the best about everyone, so much so, that he forgot that he was in a life and death power struggle.

Spiritual renewal heightens our awareness that we are in a struggle that is not just against flesh and blood, "but against the rulers, against the authorities, against the powers of this dark world and the against the spiritual forces of evil in the heavenly realms" (Eph. 6:12). It is wise to be discerning and not naively trusting in people. Jesus exemplified this cautious reserve when he refused to entrust himself to people, because he knew human nature (John 2:24). The apostle Paul emphasized that the grace that brings salvation teaches us to say "'No' to ungodliness and worldly passions, and to live self-controlled, upright and godly lives in this present age, while we wait for the blessed hope..." (Titus 2:11). This requires diligence to uphold what is good and vigilance to put down what is evil. For the sake of others, as well as ourselves, we cannot afford to be like Gedaliah. Jesus' warned, "I am sending you out like sheep among wolves. Therefore be as shrewd as snakes and as innocent as doves" (Matt.10:16). We need to be on guard and heed the apostle's admonition, "Do not be overcome by evil, but overcome evil with good" (Rom.12:21).

Spiritual renewal follows the will of God (42:1-43:13).

The man of the hour was Johanan who rescued all of the people that Ishmael had captured at Mizpah (41:11-17). Fearing retaliation from Babylon for Ishmael's assassination of Gedaliah, Johanan planned to lead the people to Egypt. But before leaving, he "and all the people from the least to the greatest approached Jeremiah the prophet and said to him, "Please hear our petition and pray to the Lord your God for this entire remnant. For as you now see, though we were once many, now only a few are left. Pray that the Lord your God will tell us where we should go and what we should do" (42:2). Unlike Gedaliah who did not consult Jeremiah when he should have, Johanan took the initiative to ask for prayer and to seek the Lord's will. Jeremiah took their request seriously, saying, "I have heard you. I will certainly pray to the Lord your God as you have requested; I will tell you everything the Lord says and will keep nothing back from you" (42:4). They appear to respond with utmost sincerity, saying, "May the Lord be a true and faithful witness against us if we do not act in accordance with everything the Lord your God sends you to tell us. Whether it is favorable or unfavorable, we will obey the Lord our God, to whom we are sending you, so that it will go well with us, for we will obey the Lord our God" (42:5-6). Tragically, however, their piety was a cover for wilful disobedience. They approached Jeremiah with all the right words, but it soon became evident that their minds were made up.

For ten days Jeremiah prayed and the people waited for a word from the Lord. Johanan must have felt that with each passing day the danger increased of the Babylonian army overrunning them. Finally on the tenth day, Jeremiah called the people together and delivered what the Lord had made clear to him. The message of the Lord Almighty was emphatic, "Stay in this land...Do not be afraid of the king of Babylon." The warning was absolutely clear, "All who are determined to go to Egypt to settle there you will die by the sword, famine and plague" (42:7-22). By the end of the message it became clear to Jeremiah that the people were determined to go to Egypt. They wanted the will of God in theory but not in practice. Instead of trusting that the Lord would protect them, they wanted to escape to Egypt. The drive for self-preservation and the appeal of the land of Egypt was too great for them. In their arrogance, they accused Jeremiah of being set up by Baruch. "You are lying!" they said. "The Lord our God has not sent you to say, 'You must not go to Egypt to settle there.' But Baruch son of Neriah is inciting you against us to hand us over to the Babylonians, so that they may kill us or carry us into exile into Babylon" (43:2-3).

After all his years of faithful ministry, impeccable integrity and fulfilled prophecy, how could anyone accuse Jeremiah of lying? He was the one prophet whose word had consistently been proven true. Time and again he delivered the Word of the Lord even though doing so endangered his life. Nevertheless he was led away to Egypt to finish his days in a foreign land among a condemned people. But even though the people turned against Jeremiah and made their accusations personal and vindictive, he remained focused on the message of the Lord. Their disobedience, hypocrisy and duplicity did not break his spirit or silent his prophetic voice. Even at the entrance to Pharaoh's palace in Tahpanhes, Jeremiah was still giving object lessons and declaring the Word of the Lord (43:8-13). If there is anyone who exemplifies what it means to seek and obey the will of the Lord it is Jeremiah. While others paid lip service to the Lord, Jeremiah loved the Lord his God with all his heart, mind, strength, and soul. It is so easy to use a show of piety to cover up our selfishness and wilful disobedience that we often fool ourselves.

Spiritual renewal is faithful to the end (44:1-30).

There was no retirement for Jeremiah. His final years in Egypt were disheartening. After a long and grueling prophetic ministry in Jerusalem, he experienced no relief in Egypt. In some ways the last chapter of his life is reminiscent of the beginning of his prophetic ministry when he attacked the pagan rituals performed in Jerusalem. After all these years the people were still practicing pagan religious rituals and Jeremiah was still tasked with declaring the Word of the Lord, saying, "Do not do this detestable thing that I hate!" (44:4). Only now, the people substituted Egyptian paganism for Canaanite practices. More than thirty years of prophetic ministry, followed by God's devastating judgment against Judah, showed little or no impact on the Jewish remnant in Egypt. If anything the refugees were convinced that their suffering was due to the fact that they had not been "burning incense to the Queen of Heaven and pouring out drink offerings to her" (44:18). They looked back at Manasseh's fifty-five year rule as a "golden age"of prosperity, power and pleasure.

The Jews became convinced in Egypt that fidelity to Yahweh was a big mistake. It was better to be broad minded and religiously inclusive, than to be narrowly focused on Yahweh. This must have been devastating to Jeremiah, but he did not give up or give in. Even when the Jews throughout Egypt agreed together to reject Jeremiah, saying, "We will not listen to the message you have spoken to us in the name of the Lord!" the prophet continued to deliver the Word of the Lord. Jeremiah had the last word, because he preached the Living Word:

> "Go ahead then, do what you promised! Keep your vows! But hear the Word of the Lord, all Jews living in Egypt: 'I swear by my great name,' says the Lord, 'that no one from Judah living anywhere in Egypt will ever again invoke my name or swear, 'As surely as the Sovereign Lord lives.'" (44:25-26).

Jeremiah's life reminds us that *faithfulness to the end authenticates faith from the beginning.* He ended his ministry in virtually the same way he began, by denouncing idolatry, upholding the truth of Yahweh, and calling for basic obedience.

Baruch means *Blessed*

In a small epilogue at the end of this chronicle of spiritual resistance, Baruch offers a personal note dated from the fourth year of Jehoiakim (605 BC). He records an exchange between Jeremiah and himself that occurred around the time he prepared a scroll of Jeremiah's dictation and read it at the temple (36:1-32). The bond between these two men must have been close. When Jeremiah purchased a field in Anathoth from his cousin, he entrusted the land deed to Baruch as a pledge that God would restore the land (32:11-16). When Johanan and the rest of the refugees rejected Jeremiah's counsel, they blamed it on Baruch, possibly because he had ties to the Jewish exiles in Babylon. Baruch's brother was a "staff officer" to the king (51:59). In any case their relationship was perceived as close by friends and enemies alike (43:3).

Through the years Baruch had risked his life to deliver Jeremiah's message because he believed it was the Word of the Lord. He was a faithful assistant and friend and more than likely had a hand in how the book of Jeremiah was arranged. If anyone has the reputation for enduring a long-term lonely ministry it is Jeremiah, but even he did not go it alone. The Lord provided in Baruch a close friend, a colleague and a fellow-sufferer. In a word Baruch was a blessing to Jeremiah. Together they remind us of Jesus' words, "For where two or three come together in my name, there I am with them" (Matt.18:20).

Baruch's personal word, here at the end, is both endearing and instructive. He reflects on the time he was at the end of his rope and he complained to the Lord God in the presence of Jeremiah. "Woe to me!" Baruch lamented. "The Lord has added sorrow to my pain; I am worn out with groaning and find no rest" (45:3). He then recalls Jeremiah's forceful spiritual direction, "This is what the Lord says: I will overthrow what I have built and uproot what I have planted, throughout the land. Should you then seek great things for yourself? Seek them not. For I will bring disaster on all people, declares the Lord, but wherever you go I will let you escape with your life" (45:4-5).

Early in their ministry together, Jeremiah reminded Baruch that their lives were part of God's great Salvation History story. They had been given a difficult mission, one that excluded selfish ambition and private agendas. Baruch may have been comparing his role as Jeremiah's scribe to that of his brother who was a public official. Be that as it may, Jeremiah stressed that their personal stories were only important insofar as they related to God's redemptive story. Baruch was being asked to put his life on the line, even as he was being promised that God would protect his life. Jeremiah reminded Baruch that it was not in spite of but because of a long and difficult ministry that he was blessed. The same holds true today for the disciples of the Lord Jesus.

9. A Prophet to the Nations

"This is the Word of the Lord that came to Jeremiah
the prophet concerning the nations: Concerning
Egypt.....concerning the Philistines ... concerning
Moab ... concerning the Ammonites ...concerning
Edom ... concerning Damascus ... concerning Kedar
and the kingdoms of Hazor ... concerning Babylon."
                                                Jeremiah 46-50

Jeremiah worked so long and hard in Jerusalem that we might forget that he was appointed by the Lord "as a prophet to the nations" (1:5). Any thought that Jeremiah represented some isolated ethnic deity rather than the Sovereign Lord of the nations ought to be dispelled by his powerful message to the surrounding nations. His familiarity with the nations is reflected in his thorough and detailed knowledge of each nation. Jeremiah was a prophet, not a tourist, called to deliver sweeping messages of judgment. The God of Israel was none other than the Lord Almighty whose rule continues to extend over all the nations.

A Global Village

Jeremiah's message of judgment was carefully crafted to capture the brave bravado of nationalistic zeal and the abject horror of utter defeat. He prophesied that regal warriors would be routed and crushed, proud kings humiliated and forced into exile. He used national idols, like the serpent, to depict a defeated Egypt slithering away (46:22). He likened an invading army to an overflowing torrent that would overwhelm the Philistines and render them so helpless that even fathers could not help their children (47:3). He prophesied that Moab's prime real estate, situated proudly on an elevated plateau east of the Dead Sea, would be reduced to rubble. Like a vintage wine she would be poured out and her wine jugs smashed. He exposed Moab's pride, Ammon's materialism, and Edom's conceit. He described the once proud capital city of Syria, Damascus, as a feeble, panic-stricken woman with no place to turn. Even the nomadic tribes of Kedar and Hazor could not find refuge in the caves against Nebuchadnezzar's advancing army. And Elam, located in modern Iran, east of Babylon, would be defenseless against an army that swept through like a hurricane, scattering, shattering and destroying everything in its path.

Jeremiah had been announcing international judgment on the global village for decades. In this final section, his prophecy against Egypt dates from 605 BC and his prophecy against Babylon was delivered in 594 BC (51:59). From a secular point-of-view Jeremiah had no platform from which to pronounce these judgments and in the eyes of the world he must have been a voice crying in the wilderness. He had no miracles to his credit to substantiate his credentials as the Lord's prophet. The fact that he was from a small, inconsequential nation that mattered little on the world scene, did not stop him from doing what the Lord had called him to do, even though it put his own life at grave risk.

His message against Babylon was as long as his messages against all the other nations combined. Babylon, the onetime agent of God's wrath, "the hammer of the whole earth" (50:23), and "a gold cup in the Lord's hand" (51:7), was now slated for the full fury of the Lord's vengeance.

We tend to think that seeing the world as a global village is a recent phenomenon inspired by modern technologies, world travel and global communications, but Jeremiah's global village was neither supersonic nor wireless. It was not modeled after the Tower of Babel, nor was there a global economy driving Jeremiah's global village. In Jeremiah's world-view, human solidarity was ultimately all about the politics of the Kingdom of God. His vision of the global village was shaped by the nature of God and the reality of salvation history. Even though he remained in the vicinity of Jerusalem for almost his entire life, until he was taken against his will to Egypt where he finished out his ministry (43:6), Jeremiah's ministry was anything but provincial or parochial. His ministry was both incarnational and global, meaning that he embodied the message of God in every dimension of his personal life and then consistently applied the Lord's message to the nations.

For Jeremiah there was an inseparable seamless connection between personal spirituality and global politics. The God of Israel was not a local deity sponsored by an ethnic religion, but the Lord Almighty, the sovereign God of the nations, who held the nations to account. His entire life was governed by this deeply personal and truly global mission, which was declared by God at the outset of work, "See, today I appoint you over nations and kingdoms to uproot and tear down, to destroy and overthrow, to build and to plant" (1:10; see 31:28; 45:4).

Since Jeremiah's world-view was shaped by the Sovereign Lord he was spared the feelings of humiliation and defeatism that often afflict an oppressed people. Ethnic pride and political nationalism had no place in his vision because his global perspective issued from divine revelation. He was able to pronounce God's judgment against the nations with a judicial objectivity free of personal animosity and racial superiority because he was convinced of God's ultimate control over history. Jeremiah's hopeful vision of the future spared him the trauma of judging life solely on the basis of his personal experience of pain and injustice. His theology of the end times found passionate expression in his poetic description of the trauma of the human condition apart from God and the utter necessity of divine judgment.

The Poetry of Judgment

Hebrew Professor John Bright finds in these chapters (46-51) "some of the finest poetry in the entire prophetic canon."[xxiv] Jeremiah's primary concern was to communicate the *experience* of judgment. The *reasons* for judgment can be found embedded in his vivid description of the horrors of war. Instead of a pedantic description of wrongs or an indictment of offenses, Jeremiah chose to portray horrific battle scenes. The modern equivalent might be the first twenty minutes of Stephen Spielberg's *Saving Private Ryan*. In his message "against the army of Pharaoh Neco king of Egypt," Jeremiah described one of the most decisive battles in Egyptian history, the battle at Carchemish on the Euphrates River (the modern Jerablus), when Nebuchadnezzar defeated the Egyptian army in 605 BC.[xxv] This was the same Pharaoh who killed King Josiah at Megiddo four years earlier (609 BC).

Jeremiah has the Egyptian commander barking out orders one minute and describing a full scale rout the next,

> "'Present arms!
> March to the front!
> Harness the horses!
> Up on the saddles!
> Battle formation! Helmets on,
> spears sharpened, armor in place!'
> But what's this I see?
> They're scared out of their wits!
> They break ranks and run for cover.
> Their soldiers panic.
> They run this way and that,
> stampeding blindly.
> It's total chaos, total confusion, danger everywhere!"
> God's Decree.
> (46:3-5; The Message)

No one was swift enough, strong enough, or skilled enough to escape the Lord's day of vengeance. The Egyptian army went up in smoke like a huge sacrifice on the banks of the Euphrates. There was nothing available, certainly no balm in Gilead, that would heal their wound or take away their shame (46:6-12). Jeremiah's focus on the catastrophic experience almost ignores the reasons for judgment, except for a statement that comes at the center of his first poem against Egypt that says,

> "Who is this like the Nile in flood?
> Like its streams torrential?
> Why, it's Egypt like the Nile in flood,
> like its streams torrential,
> Saying, 'I'll take over the world.

I'll wipe out cities and peoples.'"
(46:7-8; The Message).

The second poem describes Egypt's futile last stand against Nebuchadnezzar's invasion (46:13-26). The call to battle can be heard throughout the land to rally the troops, but it is pointless because Egypt's warriors are powerless against the Babylonian army. "They cannot stand, for the Lord will push them down. They will stumble repeatedly; they will fall over each other....They will exclaim, 'Pharaoh king of Egypt is only a loud noise; he has missed his opportunity" (46:15-17). Egypt is like "a beautiful sleek heifer attacked by a horsefly from the north!" Egypt is like a hissing snake fleeing from an advancing army. The "Daughter of Egypt" is like a woman "raped by vandals from the north"(46:20,22,24 The Message). We get the picture of devastating judgment. Jeremiah's postscript summarizes the Lord Almighty's verdict and then adds a single line that hints of Egypt's future restoration, which reads, "'Later, however, Egypt will be inhabited as in times past,' declares the Lord" (46:26). Even though the judgment theme dominates, there is more to the story of Egypt than judgment. She still has a future in God's plan. The last word on Egypt is filled with grace.

Gospel Parallels

This single line of hope for Egypt precedes Jeremiah's message of consolation for Israel. For in the end their destinies are tied together. They are united in the history of redemption. God will bless the nations through Israel by sending his Anointed One, through whom "all peoples on earth will be blessed" (Gen. 12:3). What Jeremiah said to

Israel could very well have been repeated after each of his messages to the surrounding nations. The lines of hope Jeremiah threw out to the surrounding nations are tied to the destiny of Jacob. So when he concluded his judgment pronouncement against Moab by saying, "Yet I will restore the fortunes of Moab in days to come," Jeremiah was convinced that such a promise rested on the destiny of Israel (48:47). And when he concluded his judgment pronouncement against Ammon by saying, "Yet afterward, I will restore the fortunes of the Ammonites,' declares the Lord," the prophet believed that Ammon's future and Israel's future were linked in God's redemptive plan (49:6; see 49:39). The message of hope followed Jeremiah's first message of judgment as a comforting reminder of Israel's strategic redemptive place among *all* the nations.

Jeremiah's message of blessing was a precursor to the first word of the Gospel. Repeatedly, Jesus began his encounters with the reassuring phrase "Do not be afraid." This was not a polite attempt to put people at ease in his presence, but a bold pronouncement of lasting hope grounded in God's Salvation History. The first word of the Gospel and Jeremiah's word of consolation have the same source and meaning. "Do not fear, O Jacob my servant; do not be dismayed, O Israel," is not a passing line of nationalistic rhetoric, but a powerful reminder of God's covenant with Israel to bless the nations.

The second parallel between Jeremiah's message of hope and Jesus' Gospel message is the description of what we are saved out of. Jeremiah declared the Lord's promise, "I will surely save you out of a distant place, your descendants from the land of their exile. Jacob will again have peace and security, and no one will make him afraid" (46:27). Both Israel and the Church are saved "out of a distant place." Just how "distant" can be judged from Jeremiah's poetic description of the surrounding nations. Moab, located east of the Dead Sea on a high fertile plateau, was known for her lush vines and wine production. Moab had placed her trust in riches and enjoyed a luxuriate lifestyle. She was complacent and had her full of wine. Like Pharaoh she also exuded pride. "We have heard of Moab's pride," preached Jeremiah, "her overweening pride and conceit, her pride and arrogance and the haughtiness of her heart. I know her insolence but it is futile" (48:29-30). Because of this pride Jeremiah rained down the vocabulary of judgment to describe what would happen to every city of Moab. She would be ruined, disgraced, shattered, silenced, broken and laid waste (48:1-10) and the Lord, far from delighting in this judgment, would wail, cry out, moan and weep for Moab (48:31-36).

Idolatry and greed made Ammon and Edom "distant places" as well. But the terror of the Lord was about to silence their boasting and shatter their trust in riches. There was no place for Damascus, Kedar and Hazor to hide from God's judgment, for even though "'you build your nest as high as the eagle's, from there I will bring you down,' declares the Lord" (49:16). Jeremiah's poetic description of judgment renders all the "distant places" traumatized and terror struck. Israel's neighbors from Egypt to Elam are helpless to defend themselves or escape the wrath of God. Nevertheless, Yahweh promised, "I will surely save you out of a distant place....Though I completely destroy all the nations among which I scatter you, I will not completely destroy you" (46:28).

These "distant places" out of which Israel was to be saved parallel the rescue of believers from a world of pride, greed, idolatry and sloth. Jeremiah's description of the nations illustrates the nature of worldliness and "the basic principles of this world" (Col. 2:20). Whether speaking of political powers or individual selves, the fallen human condition manifests itself in "sexual immorality, impurity, lust, evil desires and greed, which is idolatry." It is because of this fallen evil world that Paul declared, "the wrath of God is coming" (Col. 3:5-6). This is the world of trouble that Jesus Christ has overcome (John 16:33), the "distant place" where the believer is *in* the world, but no more *of* world than Christ is *of* the world (John 17:14-16). It is this world of sin and death that Christ's followers are called out of and sent back into for Christ's sake (John 17:18).

James warned us to keep our distance from this "distant place" when he said that "friendship with the world is hatred toward God" (James 4:4). And John declared, "Do not love the world or anything in the world. If anyone loves the world, the love of the Father is not in him. For everything in the world—the cravings of sinful man, the lust of the eyes and the boasting of what he has and does—comes not from the Father but from the world. The world and its desires pass away, but the man who does the will of God lives forever" (1 John 2:15-17). Peter reminds us that those who are "called out of darkness into his wonderful light" are "aliens and strangers in the world" and urged "to abstain from sinful desires" (1 Pet. 2:9-11).

A third parallel can be found between Jeremiah's message of consolation and Jesus' great commission. Even as Israel existed among the surrounding nations, so the Church exists in the world. If the people of God were extracted from the world, the world would be left behind, but neither in the case of Israel nor the Church has this ever been the plan of God. Israel, scattered among the nations, parallels the church commissioned to "make disciples of all nations" (Matt. 28:19). Israel as a faithful remnant set the stage for the emergence of the world-wide Body of Christ.

The Lord's promise to Israel, "Do not fear, O Jacob my servant, for I am with you," parallels the Lord's promise to the Church, "Surely I will be with you always, to the very end of the age" (Matt. 28:20). The Word of the Lord, through the prophet Jeremiah, parallels the letters to the seven church recorded in the apostle John's Revelation. "Though I completely destroy all the nations among which I scatter you, I will not completely destroy you. I will discipline you but only with justice; I will not let you go entirely unpunished" (46:28). The Church will not be saved from the tribulation, but through the tribulation. The trajectory of Jeremiah's New Covenant prophecy reaches all the way to the end and gathers up the promises made to the faithful remnant *in Christ.* Zion will not be a geographic destination in the Holy Land but a relational congregation before the Holy One. Jeremiah prophesied better than he knew, but his prophecy applies to the Church today better than we know. Time has not eclipsed his message, but has only served to heighten it.

> "'In those days, at that time,' declares the Lord, 'the people of Israel and the people of Judah together will go in tears to seek the Lord their God. They will ask the way to Zion and turn their faces toward it. They will come and bind themselves to the Lord in an everlasting covenant that will not be forgotten'" (50:4-5).

The Lord of the Nations

The tenth and final nation on Jeremiah's judgment list was Babylon. The hammer that God used to shatter the whole earth was next in line to become broken and shattered (50:23). The Babylonian army towered above the Egyptian army like a steep mountain (46:18) and swept over the Philistines with their galloping stallions and iron chariots (47:3). They swooped down on Moab like an eagle (48:40) and reduced Ammon to "a mound of ruins" (49:2). They struck such fear in the heart of Edom's warriors that they became like women in labor (49:22) and they burned Damascus down to the ground (49:27). Even the nomadic peoples of Kedar and Hazor were not safe from the Babylonian terror and Elam's bow was no match for Babylonian might (49:29,35).

Babylon has ravaged the nations, but what she has done to Israel deserved special indictment. Babylon's fate was sealed because she had pillaged Yahweh's inheritance (50:11), crushed his bones (50:17), oppressed his people (50:33), and committed violence against Zion (51:24,35). She "defied the Lord, the Holy One of Israel. Therefore, her young men will fall in the streets; all her soldiers will be silenced in that day" (50:30). Jeremiah announced, "The Lord will take vengeance, vengeance for his temple" (51:11). "Babylon must fall because of Israel's slain, just as the slain in all the earth have fallen because of Babylon" (51:49). The Lord Almighty was lifting up his banner over Babylon and announcing to the nations that Babylon's idols, including Bel, the title of the storm-god Enlil and Marduk, king of the gods and head of the Babylonian pantheon, were to be put to shame (50:2).

The once proud superpower was to be reduced to a wasteland (50:39). "...The boast of the whole earth seized!" Jeremiah exclaimed. "What a horror Babylon will be among the nations! The sea will rise over Babylon; its roaring waves will cover her....and the wall of Babylon will fall" (51:41-44).

The once invincible Babylonian army will cower behind their barricades, terrified by "waves of enemies" who will rage against them like a tidal wave (51:55). The Lord Almighty was going to hold nothing back. "The Lord has opened his arsenal and brought out the weapons of his wrath, for the Sovereign Lord has work to do in the land of the Babylonians" (50:25). God was sending "a nation from the north," also referred to as "an alliance of great nations from the land of the north," and "a great nation and many kings...from the ends of the earth," who will "chase Babylon from its land in an instant" (50:3,9,41,44).

The timing of Jeremiah's prophesies against Babylon can be dated in 594/3 B.C. when Baruck's brother Seraiah, a staff officer to Zedekiah king of Judah, read them aloud in Babylon. During this period between the two exiles, Zedekiah must have been forced by Nebuchadnezzar to come to Babylon to pledge his loyalty. At the time, Babylon dominated the world and showed no signs of loosening its grip. We are left with the picture of Seraiah reading Jeremiah's scroll aloud, presumably to the Hebrew delegation that had traveled with him from Jerusalem. When he finished, as ordered by Jeremiah, he pronounced this verdict: "O Lord, you have said you will destroy this place, so that neither person nor animal will live in it; it will be desolate forever." He then tied a stone to the document and threw it into the Euphrates, saying, "So will Babylon sink to rise no more because of the disaster I will bring upon her. And her people will fall" (51:62-64).

A century earlier Babylon topped Isaiah's hit list as well. Even though Babylon was then only an emerging superpower and Assyria was Israel's immediate threat, Babylon would eventually conquer Judah and force the Jews into exile. Ever since the Tower of Babel, Babylon has symbolized the solidarity of worldly principalities and powers. Isaiah called Babylon "the jewel of kingdoms," and his description of the boastful Babylonian spirit recalls the people of Shinar:

> "You said in your heart, 'I will ascend to heaven; I will raise my throne above the stars of God; I will sit enthroned on the mount of assembly, on the utmost heights of the sacred mountain. I will ascend above the tops of the clouds; I will make myself like the Most High.' But you are brought down to the grave, to the depths of the pit" (14:13-15; see 13:19).

Isaiah pictured Babylon as an emerging threat and Jeremiah described Babylon as a reigning superpower. Both prophets saw Babylon as the embodiment of human success turned against the Lord God. Some seven hundred years after Jeremiah, the Apostle John used Babylon to symbolize not only the Roman Empire, but every secular and spiritual power that set itself up against the Kingdom of God. Down through the ages God has pronounced judgment against the spirit of Babylon. "Woe! Woe, O great city, O Babylon, city of power! In one hour your doom has come!" (Rev. 18:10). The apostle John saw ancient Babylon as the prototype for the first century Roman Empire and he used the language of Isaiah and Jeremiah to prophecy against Rome. Jeremiah's message continues to have special relevance for today's representation of the people of God, the Church. Israel's vulnerability among the nations and her centrality in God's redemptive plan is true today for the Body of Christ. Like Isaiah, Jeremiah offered a powerful vision of what it means to pray, "Your Kingdom come, Your will be done, on earth as it is in heaven" (Matt. 6:10).

Jeremiah's message of judgment remains a forceful reminder to the Church of just how desperate the human condition is apart from God. For all those who place their trust in themselves are doomed to experience the horror of God's judgment. Those who trust in the idols of success, sex, and self for salvation will meet with the same fate Jeremiah pronounced against the nations. It is a grave mistake to dismiss God's judgment as an anachronistic Old Testament theme. Jesus spoke of hell (Matt. 5:29-30; 10:28) and referred to a place of utter darkness, "where there will be weeping and gnashing of teeth" (Matt. 8:12). He said that it would be more bearable for Sodom and Gomorrah on the day of judgment than for those who reject the gospel (Matt. 10:15). He envisioned a fiery and painful final end to all who rejected the witness of the Spirit and persisted in their evil ways (Matt. 12:31-33; 13:42). At the end of the age, Jesus said, "angels will come and separate the wicked from the righteous and throw them into the fiery furnace, where there will be weeping and gnashing of teeth" (Matt. 13:50; 24:51). It is impossible to believe in salvation and reject judgment because the two are inseparable, as the apostle Paul stated so forcefully, "For those who are self-seeking and who reject the truth and follow evil, there will be wrath and anger. There will be trouble and distress for every human being who does evil: first for the Jew, then for the Gentile; but glory, honor and peace for everyone who does good: first for the Jew, then for the Gentile. For God does not show favoritism" (Rom. 2:8-11).

Jeremiah's prophecies bring the message home that the Lord will judge his people, and as the author of Hebrews wrote, "It is a dreadful thing to fall into the hands of the living God" (Heb. 10:31). The difference between Jeremiah's message and Jesus' gospel is one of emphasis. The truth of divine judgment and salvation remain the same, but since Jesus has come the accent has shifted to the good news of salvation. The Gospel assumes the truth of divine judgment and emphasizes the truth of the gift of salvation: "For God did not send his Son into the world to condemn the world, but to save the world through him. Whoever believes in him is not condemned, but whoever does not believe stands condemned already because he has not believed in the name of God's one and only Son" (John 3:17-18; see 12:47-50). The Gospel of Jesus assumes all that Jeremiah prophesied on judgment and then elaborates on Jeremiah's single lines of hope and restoration (46:26; 48:47; 49:6; 49:39). What Jeremiah said about Israel being saved "out of a distant place" (46:27-28) and Israel being bound "to the Lord in an everlasting covenant" (50:4-5) is the truth the Gospel builds on and commends to a lost world. Jeremiah looked forward to that day when there would be freedom from oppression and rest throughout the land, because "their Redeemer is strong; the Lord Almighty is his name" (50:33-34). Inherent in his message of hope is the Gospel of the Lord Jesus Christ.

10. A Gethsemane Life

*"I remember my affliction and my wandering, the
bitterness and the gall. I well remember them, and my
soul is downcast within me. Yet this I call to mind
and therefore I have hope: Because of the Lord's great
love we are not consumed, for his compassions never
fail. They are new every morning; great is thy
faithfulness."* Lamentations 3:19-23

Jeremiah's forty years of heart-breaking, life-threatening
ministry is an inspiring, yet sobering, reminder to the
followers of Jesus of the cost of obedience. Ever true to
the Word of the Lord, Jeremiah obeyed Yahweh. He got
himself ready and stood for four decades, declaring
whatever the Lord commanded him to say (1:17). He faced
Judah's evil kings, lying prophets, bad priests, plotting
relatives and foreign kings, without giving in and yielding
an inch. He delivered the Lord's scathing message of
judgment and experienced the full brunt of Judah's
rejection of God. His own family betrayed him, and the
religious and political leaders tried to kill him. Yet his life
testified to the Yahweh's promise, "Today I have made you
a fortified city, an iron pillar and bronze wall to stand
against the whole land" (1:18).

God's protection, however, did not spare Jeremiah intense and agonizing grief. This stalwart prophet, pastor and poet, was a man of deep feelings and a broken heart. He preached judgment with tears: "Oh, that my head were a spring of water and my eyes a fountain of tears! I would weep day and night for the slain of my people" (9:1). He was bold in public; he wept in private: "I will weep in secret because of your pride; my eyes will weep bitterly, overflowing with tears, because the Lord's flock will be taken captive" (13:17). Because the Lord had withdrawn his blessing, his love and his pity from the people, Jeremiah was ordered to do so as well (16:5). He remained single, refused to attend funerals, rejected hospitality, and showed up at the temple to do battle. Even his loneliness sent a message. Jeremiah didn't sermonize, he embodied the Word of the Lord in his life and character. He was not the Incarnate One, but he lived an incarnational life.

Jeremiah was a parable of Jesus, 600 years before Jesus. His physical, emotional and spiritual suffering causes us to reflect on Jesus' agony in Gethsemane and his suffering on the cross. Jeremiah experienced in his own mind, body and soul the judgment of God that Judah deserved. In a courageous act of willed passivity he walked alongside a rebellious and disobedient people through the valley of despair and helped them to grieve their loss and interpret their suffering. He gave true words and perspective to their lament and challenged them to grapple with the validity of God's judgment. He taught them how to submit to God's justice and judgment and work through their grief to an enduring hope in God's great faithfulness.

In the Pit

It may be difficult to determine the low point in Jeremiah's career because he had so many. Was it when he learned that his family was plotting against him (11:19) or when Pashhur, the chief officer of the temple, had him beaten and put in the stocks (20:1-2)? Was it when the Lord told him not to marry and to live as a social outcast (16:2-9) or was it when "the priests, the prophets and all the people seized him and said, 'You must die!'" (26:8-9)? Was it when Hananiah publicly accused and humiliated Jeremiah and broke the yoke he had around his neck (28:2-10) or was it when he hid from King Jehoiakim after the king cut up his scroll and threw the pieces into the fire (36:19-17)?

Of all the trials that Jeremiah experienced, the episode that may capture the depth of his suffering best was when he was lowered into a muddy cistern and left to die. He had been telling the people what he had told them all along, "This is what the Lord says: 'Whoever stays in this city will die by the sword, famine or plague, but whoever goes over to the Babylonians will live. He will escape with his life; he will live'" (38:2). Many of Jerusalem's leaders judged this now familiar message a treacherous betrayal and concluded, "This man should be put to death. He is discouraging the soldiers who are left in the city, as well as all the people, by the things he is saying to them. This man is not seeking the good of these people but their ruin" (38:4). King Zedekiah answered these false accusations against Jeremiah by abdicating his responsibility. "He is in your hands. The king can do nothing to oppose you" (38:5).

One cannot read this without thinking of the false accusations that were hurled at Jesus and recalling Pilate's abdication of responsibility (Matt. 27:24). For Jesus it meant going to the cross; for Jeremiah it meant being lowered into a muddy cistern. We have no idea how long Jeremiah was left in the cistern but long enough for one of the officials in the royal palace by the name of Ebed-Melech, a Cushite (Ethiopian) to worry about his survival, and long enough for Zedekiah to regain some sense of responsibility. At some risk to his own career, Ebed-Melech approached the king saying, "My lord the king, these men have acted wickedly in all they have done to Jeremiah the prophet. They have thrown him into a cistern, where he will starve to death when there is no longer any bread in the city" (38:9).

Thankfully Zedekiah listened to reason and ordered Ebed-Melech to take thirty men and "lift Jeremiah the prophet out of the cistern before he dies" (38:10). The fact that Ebed-Melech made an effort to pad the rope with old rags and clothing, indicated that Jeremiah had become emaciated and too weak to support himself as they hoisted him out of the well. It must have been a dramatic moment when Jeremiah was lifted out of the cistern barely alive, even as it was when Jesus' body was lifted down from the cross. Ebed-Melech must have handled the prophet with the utmost care and respect, even as we picture Joseph of Arimathea carefully handling his Savior's body (Matt. 27:57-60).

In that miserable, muddy pit Jeremiah was forced to face the imminent reality of death, but nothing of his will and purpose changed. He remained faithful to his calling. His enemies considered him as good as dead, but his resolve remained undiminished and his courage undaunted. Even in the pit he was "as impregnable as a castle, immovable as a steel post, and as solid as a concrete wall" (1:18; The Message). As near as we can tell, Jeremiah's ministry didn't skip a beat. He went right on proclaiming the Word of the Lord. His faithfulness to the end proved his faith in Yahweh from the beginning. In fact if we take into account the book of *Lamentations* some of his most crucial work was yet to come. He discovered the truth, expressed by Corrie ten Boom, that no matter how deep the pit, God's love is deeper still.

In the pit and throughout his life Jeremiah showed that death no longer had mastery over him. He testified *before* Christ to the reality that was made certain in Christ. "Now if we died with Christ," wrote the apostle Paul, "we believe that we will also live with him" (Rom. 6:8). Jeremiah lived in the same freedom that is offered to the followers of Jesus Christ. Jeremiah had crucified the old self. He had died "to the basic principles of this world" and was alive to God (Col. 2:20; see Rom. 6:6). Jeremiah lived the crucified life ahead time. How much more should we who follow Christ live this way? If we can say with the apostle, "I have been crucified with Christ and I no longer live, but Christ lives in me," what can the world do to us (Gal. 2:20)?

In Lament

Those who accept the long standing tradition that *Lamentations* was written by Jeremiah have a keener sense of the importance of his continued ministry after the Babylonian army had occupied the land and deported the exiles to Babylon. The fall of Jerusalem in 587 B.C. was an event that needed to be grieved, interpreted, and reflected upon. Any impression that *Lamentations* is of marginal interest or is spiritually irrelevant is sadly mistaken. Jeremiah's work on grief was not optional, but necessary in several ways. His poetry of sorrow gave voice to nearly inexpressible anguish. He put into words what people were feeling. That in itself is a feat that requires deep empathy, spiritual skill and psychological depth. His perspective on grief also articulated the reasons for this suffering. Unless we are prepared to conclude that life is meaningless, all suffering begs for explanation and interpretation. This required Jeremiah's characteristic theological depth and insight. The prophet located the meaning of these tragic events in the larger scope of God's salvation history. His vision of hope for the future was not pie-in-the-sky idealism, but absolutely essential to the grieving process and the meaning of the suffering. At the heart of *Lamentations* lies a solid message of hope that comes through intense grief and sorrow. Jeremiah not only helped the exiles face reality, but his testimony offers invaluable spiritual direction to those who follow Christ today.

The poetic form of *Lamentations* shows the value of attending to grief in a manner that is intentional, aesthetically careful and intellectually rigorous. Jeremiah never intended his five poems to be stylistic masterpieces, mere works of art written for literary critics, but he did choose to contain his lament within a defined structure. All five poems that make up *Lamentations* have the twenty-two consonants of the Hebrew alphabet in mind. The first four poems are acrostic with each three or four line stanza in the first two poems beginning with a consecutive letter of the Hebrew alphabet. The third and fourth poems are made up of single lines grouped in threes and twos respectively, with each line beginning with the same consonant of the Hebrew alphabet. The fifth poem, a prayer, has twenty-two lines but the lines do not begin with consecutive consonants. There are a few exceptions to the stylistic structure which indicates a certain freedom within the form, but the orderly way in which this emotionally charged subject matter is treated is remarkable. For the poet, literary order paralleled theological truth. Gut-wrenching, soul-despairing grief was contained in a literary pattern that enhanced a theological perspective.

Jeremiah was an eyewitness to a national tragedy that resulted in the disastrous end to community life. We can picture Jeremiah walking the deserted streets of Jerusalem. "How deserted lies the city, once so full of people!" (Lam 1:1). Jerusalem is like a widow in mourning, a slave in chains, a humiliated outcast among the nations. Her once vibrant religious life had vanished. "The roads to Zion mourn, for no one comes to her appointed feasts. All her gateways are desolate, her priests groan, her maidens grieve, and she is in anguish" (Lam. 1:4). Because of sin, Jerusalem was in a state of utter humiliation and starvation. "Jerusalem has sinned greatly and so has become unclean" (Lam. 1:8). Jeremiah voiced Jerusalem's lament in the first person, female voice. The Daughter of Zion, the Virgin Daughter of Judah, weeps because of her sin and destitution. She cries out, "Look, O Lord, on my affliction, for the enemy has triumphed.... Look, O Lord, and consider, for I am despised... See, O Lord, how distressed I am! I am in torment within, and in my heart I am disturbed, for I have been most rebellious" (Lam. 1:9,11,20).

In the second poem Jeremiah left no doubt that the suffering of Judah was an act of God's wrath. "How the Lord has covered the Daughter of Zion with the cloud of his anger!...The Lord is like an enemy; he has swallowed up Israel...The Lord has done what he planned; he has fulfilled his word, which he decreed long ago" (Lam 2:1,5,17). The scope and intensity of Jerusalem's suffering knew no limits. "Should women eat their offspring, the children they have cared for? Should priest and prophet be killed in the sanctuary of the Lord?" (Lam. 2:20). Jeremiah's well-worn phrase "terrors on every side," was used to describe the extent of the Lord's anger (Lam. 2:22).

The third poem explores the national tragedy from a personal perspective. "I am the man who has seen affliction by the rod of his wrath. He has driven me away and made me walk in darkness rather than light; indeed, he has turned his hand against me again and again, all day long" (Lam. 3:1-3). In many ways Jeremiah had vicariously experienced the judgment of Judah ahead of time, not because of the wrath of God against him personally, but because of the ways he had been persecuted, humiliated and mistreated by those who opposed the will of God. He had born the feelings of abandonment, bitterness and hardship long before the Babylonian army showed up at the gates of Jerusalem. So he knew firsthand how to put the national calamity into words that expressed the intensity of suffering and agony of soul.

However, it is not only Jeremiah's vicarious experience of suffering that comes to mind. We cannot read this third poem of lament without thinking of Jesus' vicarious experience of suffering on the cross. There are definite affinities with Isaiah 53 and Psalm 22.[xxvi] The poem expresses the emotional and experiential side of Christ's passion. This is what Jesus felt like when "God made him who had no sin to be sin for us, so that in him we might become the righteousness of God" (2 Cor. 5:21). The connection between Jeremiah's suffering and Judah's experience underscores the prophet's empathy for his people. Whereas the personal connection between Jesus' suffering and the judgment we deserve because of our sin, underscores the vicarious sacrifice on our behalf to redeem us from our sin.

The personal and vicarious nature of the third lament gives Jeremiah's famous passage on hope special messianic significance. Jeremiah made sure to express the heart of the matter at the literal center of *Lamentations*, when he wrote,

"Because of the Lord's great love we are not consumed, for his compassions never fail. They are new every morning; great is your faithfulness. I say to myself, 'The Lord is my portion; therefore I will wait for him.' The Lord is good to those whose hope is in him, to the one who seeks him; it is good to wait quietly for the salvation of the Lord" (Lam. 3:22-26).

Along with this message of hope in the Lord's salvation is the assurance that God "will show compassion" because of his "unfailing love" and the reminder that God "does not willingly bring affliction or grief to the children of men and women" (Lam. 3:32-33; see 2 Pet. 3:9). Furthermore, the only true response to God's great faithfulness and compassion is repentance. Jeremiah admonished, "Let us examine our ways and test them, and let us return to the Lord. Let us lift up our hearts and our hands to God in heaven, and say: 'We have sinned and rebelled and you have not forgiven'" (Lam. 3:40-42). Even in the throes of intense suffering and national calamity, Jeremiah prophesied the gospel of grace:

"I called on your name, O Lord, from the depths of the pit. You heard my plea: 'Do not close your ears to my cry for relief.' You came near when I called you, and you said, 'Do not fear.' O Lord, you took up my case; you redeemed my life." (Lam. 3:55-58).

In the fourth poem, we return once again to themes of utter desperation. Extreme suffering means that even gold and gems have lost their value. Begging children are heartlessly rejected and a violent death is better than a slow death by starvation. Compassionate mothers have been reduced to eating their own children and the prophets and priests are shunned as if they were lepers. The reality is this: "The Lord has given full vent to his wrath; he has poured out his fierce anger. He kindled a fire in Zion that consumed her foundations" (Lam. 4:11). But even extreme suffering, brought on by sin and rebellion, will end and the agents of wrath will be punished. The fourth poem ends with this assurance, "O Daughter of Zion, your punishment will end; he will not prolong your exile. But, O Daughter of Edom, he will punish your sin and expose your wickedness" (Lam. 4:22).

The fifth poem is a prayer from a grieving heart to the Sovereign Lord. "Remember, O Lord, what has happened to us; look, and see our disgrace" (Lam. 5:1). The plight of Judah is reviewed and the historic, as well as personal reason for judgment is confessed, "Our fathers sinned and are no more, and we bear their punishment....Woe to us, for we have sinned!" (Lam. 5:7,16). The symbolic center of community life has become a wasteland. Mount Zion "lies desolate, with jackals prowling over it" (Lam. 5:18). The final word is a plea to the Sovereign Lord, who alone can remember, restore and renew the people of God. But the prayer is careful to assume nothing and it dreads the worst. "Restore us to yourself, O Lord, that we may return; renew our days as of old unless you have utterly rejected us and are angry with us beyond measure" (Lam. 5:21-22).

Lamentations was not only meant to shape Judah's grieving process but to provide spiritual direction for our experience of grief and suffering. By using vivid images and graphic word pictures, Jeremiah captured the experience of suffering. Instead of living in denial, he described pain with snapshots of grief and echoed the cries of anguish with tag-lines of despair. Jeremiah's poetry of grief helped to define Judah's suffering by offering an eyewitness account. Like a good doctor, he first observed his patients' suffering with astute care and precision. Then his critical observation led to a diagnosis that was not only more accurate but more acceptable to the patient.

The second lesson to be learned from Jeremiah is to understand grief and suffering in relationship to God. For Jeremiah this meant tracing the roots of the national tragedy to sin and describing God's judgment against Judah's rebellion. Jeremiah would not have been helpful to Judah in her grieving process if he had identified with her suffering but refused to talk about her sin. All suffering ought to be viewed from a God-centered perspective, because all suffering is a consequence of sin. We may have brought suffering upon ourselves because of our own sin or we may be suffering as victims of a fallen and broken world. In any case, the roots of suffering need to be seen in the light of God's will and in the truth of God's Word. Suffering ought to move us to God, causing us to become dependent upon his love and mercy, so that we can either repent of our evil ways or be empowered to resist evil. Either way, Jeremiah teaches us that suffering must always be defined in relationship to God.

A third way that Jeremiah helped Judah in the grieving process was to identify with the suffering personally. He was not a detached, outside observer but a fellow sufferer. His eyewitness account was not that of journalist or an expert, but of a faithful friend. All five laments underscore Jeremiah's solidarity *with* his people. There is no sense in his laments of him feeling divorced from his people, even though he had spent a lifetime warning them of their rebellious ways and the pending consequences of their actions. In fact, his experience of unjust persecution and suffering proved invaluable in strengthening his identification with the people. Jeremiah's empathy with the people allowed him to freely use the first person singular when describing the people's suffering. He owned their grief as his own: "I remember my affliction and my wandering, the bitterness and the gall. I well remember them, and my soul is downcast within me" (Lam. 3:19-20).

As valuable as this lesson of solidarity may be, its corollary truth supersedes Jeremiah's example. Jeremiah identified with the people's grief, but Jesus went way beyond that when he bore our sin and grief on the cross. This is the crucial and often overlooked truth in understanding the grieving process from God's perspective. God's solidarity with us in our suffering is like no other. He who knew no sin became sin for us so that we might be saved from sin and death. Remarkably, the third poem in *Lamentations* can be read three ways: first as a personal description of the human condition; second, as a first person account of Jeremiah's solidarity with his people; and third, as a description of the suffering of Jesus Christ on our behalf. Any guidance on grieving or spiritual direction on suffering that ignores Christ and his Cross ignores hope and salvation.

In Hope

Jeremiah is best known for his faithful perseverance and his passionate proclamation of the Word of the Lord. He is well remembered for courageously enduring forty years of suffering and persecution in order to proclaim the truth. He is often called the weeping prophet and his name is synonymous with lamentations. It could be said that he lived a Gethsemane life. "Not my will but yours, O Lord," expressed the prayer of his life. But there is another dimension to his life that deserves to be recognized as well. Jeremiah lived into the future with passionate hope and confidence in the power of God to redeem and restore his people.

The Gospel according to Jeremiah gives us some of the best statements of hope and promise in all the Bible. Beyond his costly obedience and faithful endurance, Jeremiah expressed, at the center of his life and at the heart of his ministry, the gospel message of hope and healing. He was the prophet of God's gracious promise: "For I know the plans I have for you, plans to prosper you and not to harm you, plans to give you hope and a future" (29:11). He would be disappointed to be remembered only for his messages of judgment and lamentation, because he saw himself as the prophet of the Lord's New Covenant: "This is the covenant I will make with the house of Israel after that time. I will put my law in their minds and write it on their hearts. I will be their God and they will be my people" (31:33).

We may observe Jeremiah's life and feel sorry for him, but he didn't feel sorry for himself. Even from prison his message of hope prevailed. He was delighted to announce, "This is what the Lord says, he who made the earth, the Lord who formed it and established it—the Lord is his name: 'Call to me and I will answer you and tell you great and unsearchable things you do not know." The message of judgment he was called to give was always accompanied by God's redemptive purpose and promise. He delivered God's good news, "I will bring health and healing...I will heal my people and will let them enjoy abundant peace and security" (33:6).

Jeremiah's life was not just an endurance test and a life of suffering, but a parable of Jesus pointing forward to "The Lord Our Righteousness." Jeremiah delighted to say, ""The days are coming,' declares the Lord, 'when I will fulfill the gracious promise I made to the house of Israel and to the house of Judah. "In those days at that time I will make a righteous Branch sprout from David's line; he will do what is just and right in the land."'(33:14-16). This is why Jeremiah bought the field at Anathoth from his relative, even as the Babylonian army was besieging Jerusalem. He bought it, because he believed in the future promises of God (32:1-25). In order to understand Jeremiah in his own words, it is best to see that at the center of his difficult life was an abiding sense of the Lord's great love. At the heart of his lamentations was a song of praise: "Because of the Lord's great love we are not consumed, for his compassions never fail. They are new every morning; great is your faithfulness" (Lam. 3:22-23). What was true for Jeremiah can be true for all those who trust in Christ. Jesus is the Lord Our Righteousness.

Notes

i. Eugene Peterson, *Run with the Horses* (Downers Grove, Ill.: IVP, 1983), p. 37.

ii. Peterson, p. 50.

iii. Eugene Peterson, *The Message* (Colorado Springs: NavPress, 2002), p. 1342.

iv. G. Campbell Morgan, *Studies in the Prophecy of Jeremiah* (New York: Revell, 1931), p. 23.

v. Derek Kidner, *The Message of Jeremiah: Against Wind and Tide* (Downers Grove, Ill.: IVP, 1987), p. 31.

vi. Martin Luther, *The Bondage of the Will* (New York: Revell, 1957), p. 66.

vii. Peterson, *Run with the Horses*, p. 65.

viii. Kidner, *The Message of Jeremiah*, p. 51.

ix. John Bright, *The Anchor Bible: Jeremiah* (New York: Doubleday, 1979), p. 57

x. Eugene Peterson, *Answering God : The Psalms As Tools For Prayer* (San Francisco: Harper & Row, 1989), p. 95.

xi. Peterson, p. 98.

xii. Kidner, *The Message of Jeremiah*, p. 61.

xiii. Peterson, *Answering God*, p. 102

xiv. J. A. Thompson, *The Book of Jeremiah* (Grand Rapids: Eerdmans, 1980), p. 459.

xv. Dietrich Bonhoeffer, *Creation and Fall* (New York: SCM Press, 1959), p. 83.

xvi. R. K. Harrison, *Jeremiah & Lamentations* (Downers Grove, Ill.: IVP, 1973), p. 123.

xvii. Eugene Peterson, *Reversed Thunder: The Revelation of John & the Praying Imagination* (San Francisco: Harper & Row, 1988), p. 118.

xviii. Peterson, p. 117.

xix. Harrison, *Jeremiah & Lamentations*, pp. 136-137.

xx. John Wesley, *The Works of the Rev. John Wesley*, vol. 5 (London: Wesleyan Conference Center, 1878), p. 296.

xxi. John Stott, *Romans* (Downers Grove, Ill.: 1994), p. 33.

xxii. Karl Barth, *The Epistle to the Romans* (London: Oxford University Press, 1933), p. 454.

xxiii. John Perkins, *A Quiet Revolution* (Waco, TX: Word Books, 1976), pp. 35-36.

xxiv. Bright, *Jeremiah*, p. 307.

xxv. Thompson, *The Book of Jeremiah*, p. 688.

xxvi. Harrison, *Jeremiah & Lamentations*, p. 223.

www.ingramcontent.com/pod-product-compliance
Lightning Source LLC
Chambersburg PA
CBHW020859090426
42736CB00008B/428